KATE VENTER & EUNICE BORCHERS
Sugar Modelling

MEREHURST

Other books by Kate Venter:
Sugar Art (1984)
Sugar Decorating (1987)
Say it with Sugar (1990)
The Kate Venter Sugar Art Collection (1993)

Published 1994 by Merehurst Limited
Ferry House, 51/57 Lacy Road, Putney, London, SW15 1PR
By arrangement with Tafelberg Publishers Ltd
First edition 1994

© 1994 Tafelberg Publishers Ltd

ISBN 1 85391 408 8

Photography by Dick Bomford
Illustrations by Lynne Misicwics
Tracings by Carlo Doffizi
Cover and typography by G&G Design
Set in 10 on 12 pt Plantin Monotype Lasercomp
Printed and bound by Toppan Printing Company (H.K.) Ltd,
Hong Kong

A catalogue record for this book is available
from the British Library.

We thank Agata Pomario, Ina Goulden and Jackie Duncan for so willingly making leaves and flowers for our scenes; Irene Pienaar who gave up much time to help and was prepared to do the most boring and painstaking jobs without complaint; John Gregory for drawing up the plans for the Sacramento house; Phyllis Midlane of the Capab Wardrobe Department; and Lieske Bester who read the copy. Their contributions are greatly appreciated.

Contents

Introduction

Sugar modelling originated in Mexico, where the technique was devised to make artefacts for religious occasions. These theatrical, lifelike figures or dolls made of gum paste are dressed in period costumes and arranged in meticulously executed garden or room settings, which are frequently incorporated in or combined with structures made of pastillage. The colourful scenes, which often have a theme or tell a story, are sometimes arranged on platforms or drums set on top of cakes.

In 1979 Eunice Borchers attended a course in this exacting and fascinating technique given by Señora Marithe de Alverado. She in turn taught Kate Venter. Together they developed this technique, adapting it to local methods of cake decorating. As a highly creative form of advanced cake decorating, Mexican sugar modelling is limited only by the imagination and ability of the artist.

Novice cake decorators will find it useful to master the basic techniques as explained in *New ideas in cake design* by Eunice Borchers, and Kate Venter's *Sugar Art, Sugar Decorating, Say it with Sugar* and *The Kate Venter Sugar Art Collection*, before embarking on Mexican sugar modelling. A knowledge of garment construction and dressmaking will also be useful for the cake decorator but is not essential if the instructions are followed carefully.

Tools

Plate 1
1 Examples of torso moulds; 2 fine scissors; 3 scalpel; 4 ridged and smooth rolling pins; 5 spacers; 6 patterned ruler; 7 spacers; 8 modelling tools; 9 circular cutters in various sizes; 10 noodle machine with handle; 11 work board; 12 sponges; 13 tweezers; 14 wire cutter; 15 tracing wheel; 16 long-nosed pliers; 17 pastry cutter; 18 tracing wheel; 19 frilling tool; 20 polystyrene; 21 ruler; 22 oasis; 23 skewers; 24 pencils and pens; 25 wire; 26 brushes; 27 toothpicks; 28 spatula; 29 discs for clay gun; 30 plunger and barrel of clay gun.

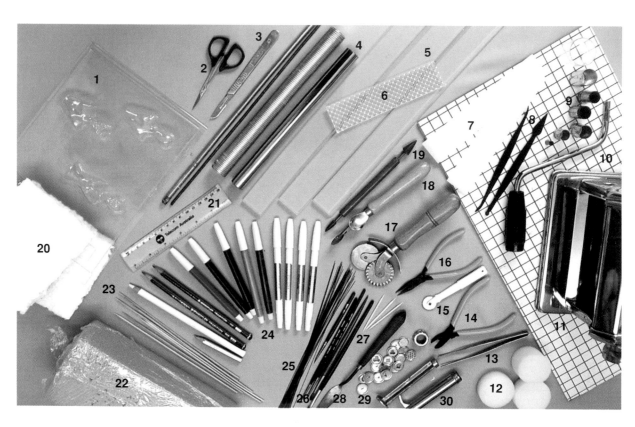

Brushes

About five round artist's brushes (Nos. 00, 0, 1, 2 and 3) are necessary for flood work and for painting flowers and other motifs. A No. 6 round brush for dusting flowers with dusting powder is also recommended. Invest in two flat-tipped brushes (Nos. 1 and 10 respectively) for rice-paper painting and dusting.

Clay gun

A clay gun as used by potters and other craftsmen is useful to make strips, ropes, etc.

Colouring

Vegetable colouring is available in liquid, powder and paste form for colouring the gum paste, pastillage, royal icing, etc., used in Mexican sugar modelling.

Cornflour

Cornflour (also known as cornstarch) is added to gum paste that is used to model figures.

Cutters

These are used for pressing out shapes such as keys, numbers, letters, petals and leaves of flower paste or plastic icing.

Dusting powders

Edible dusting powders are used in dry form to colour and give depth to designs. A wide variety of tints and shades can be obtained by mixing white and the three basic colours (red, blue and yellow). Colours can be lightened with cornflour instead of white dusting powder. A wide range of ready-mixed colours is also available from shops that stock such products.

Emery boards

Emery boards are used for smoothing the edges of pastillage pieces.

Florist's tape

Self-adhesive tape is available in different colours. A special cutter is useful for cutting the

2

tape into two, three or four equal strips. Green tape is used to cover florist's wire when making stems for flowers, leaves, etc. Florist's ribbon, available in standard widths, is used for trimming the edge of the boards. It can also be divided with a tape cutter.

Florist's wire
This is obtainable in different gauges and is used mainly for flower stems and arm attachments, and to strengthen limbs where necessary. Nos. 18, 20, 22, 24 and 26 are particularly useful.

Gum powder
Gum powder is mixed into plastic icing to make flower paste more pliable. Three kinds are available: gum tragacanth which is very expensive, carboxy-methyl cellulose (or CMC), or Tylose C 1000 P, which also results in a whiter flower paste. For the figures we have used gum tragacanth.

Knives
Three sets of knives will be enough for the beginner: a small spatula or spreader for mixing and spreading royal icing; a palette knife or artist's spatula with a blade of about 20 mm x 110 mm ($\frac{4}{5}$ in. x $4\frac{2}{5}$ in.) for lifting and handling small petals, leaves, lacework, figures, etc.; and a scalpel to cut out designs and make small or fine cuts.

Mixing bowls
Plastic bowls should not be used for mixing as they are always slightly greasy; use earthenware or glass bowls.

Modelling tools
Wooden and plastic tools are available in sets and are essential for modelling leaves, petals and figures. Pewter tools can be used instead. Marzipan and plastic icing or flower paste are used mainly for modelling work.

Moulds
Various head and figure moulds as well as moulds for columns and furniture are available in the trade. Unless otherwise stated, Barco moulds (a South African product) were used throughout this book.

Muslin cloth
Cover royal icing with damp muslin to prevent it from forming a crust. Strain the white of an egg through a piece of dry cloth to prevent threads of egg white from breaking up in the icing. Shape a piece of dry cloth into a pad and use it to smooth marzipan or plastic icing.

Noodle machine
A noodle machine is very useful but not essential, as it enables one to roll out modelling paste to the required thickness every time. Spacers will serve the same purpose with a little more trouble.

Pastry cutters
Two kinds are necessary: a pastry cutter for cutting designs out of plastic icing or flower paste and a parsley cutter to cut plastic icing or flower paste into even strips for ribbons etc.

Pens and pencils
Pink non-toxic pens, a 3H pencil and a white pencil are used for making up the faces of the figures.

Polystyrene
The stems of completed flowers may be stuck into blocks of polystyrene for drying and storage. It is also used to hold figures in position while dressing them.

Rolling pins
Ridged and smooth rolling pins in various sizes are used to roll out marzipan, plastic icing and flower paste. A small rolling pin can be made out of a piece of chrome tubing or a towel rail (about 18 mm [$\frac{4}{5}$ in.] in diameter and 150 mm [6 in.] in length).

Rulers
In addition to an ordinary ruler, a handy set of four circular dividers is available for marking cakes into various sections.

Scissors
Two pairs are necessary: an ordinary pair for cutting out paper patterns and a small pair with long, sharp, straight, thin blades for cutting the fingers of the figures.

Spacers
Spacers can be obtained in various thicknesses and lengths. Paste is rolled out between a pair for even thickness.

Stamens
These are sold in different colours and sizes in hobby and craft shops. Pearl stamens are used for jewellery and trimmings.

Sugar thermometer
Essential for preparing pastillage No. 1 and making sugar rocks.

Toothpicks and skewers
Toothpicks are used to reinforce the necks and other parts of figures, while skewers are used for the base of a woman and for men's legs.

Tracing wheel
A dressmaker's tracing wheel is useful to copy a design onto a cake and to finish off paste ribbons, imitate stitching, etc.

Turntable
This can be made of wood or stainless steel. It is not essential, as a cake or biscuit tin can be used instead, but it makes the dressing of figures easier.

Tweezers
These are indispensable for delicate work. A standard pair and a long pair with a curved point should form part of your basic equipment.

Wire cutter
This should be very sharp and of good quality to cut the wires.

Work board
This serves as a general work surface. A wooden board of 250 mm x 300 mm (10 in. x 12 in.) covered with self-adhesive plastic in a pastel chequered design is particularly useful. A rubber-backed place mat can also be used.

Recipes

In Mexico firm pound cakes are traditionally used as the base for sugar modelling, but we have found that a good fruit cake works just as well, if not better, as it improves with age. Bake and prepare a rich or a light fruit cake, as explained in Kate Venter's *Sugar Art* or *The Kate Venter Sugar Art Collection* or in Eunice Borchers' *New ideas in cake decorating*. Sponge and butter cakes are too light for this method of decorating.

Sugar modelling can be done on a platform or drum that can be placed on top of the cake and removed before the cake is cut.

Pastillage and Mexican gum paste are the two main components used in sugar modelling. As they differ vastly in strength and pliability, it is essential that they should be kept in separate, clearly marked containers to prevent confusion.

Mexican gum paste

Mexican gum paste (referred to as "paste" throughout the book) is used to make the bodies, arms and clothing of the doll-like figures as well as flowers, accessories and trimmings. The paste is very pliable and ideally suited to the purpose. Allow the bodies to dry for at least three days before making up the faces and dressing the figures. If the weather is very hot it is advisable to prick the bodies with a toothpick where they will be covered later with clothing. This will prevent the outside of the figure from drying too quickly before the inside can dry, which may cause cracks.

250 g   (1½ cups)   icing sugar
15 ml   (1 level tablespoon)   gum tragacanth
45-60 ml   (3-4 tablespoons)   cold water
5 ml   (1 teaspoon)   heavy glucose
15 ml (1 tablespoon) cornflour (for bodies only)

Sift the icing sugar and gum tragacanth together into a large bowl. Make a well in the sugar mixture and pour in the water. Drop the glucose into the water. Mix well with the fingertips until soft, then mix to a soft dough. Leave for half an hour to set. If too sticky, add more sugar; if too stiff, add more water drop by drop. Keep working the paste until pliable and elastic. Add the cornflour only if the paste will be used for the bodies of figures.

Use the paste immediately or the same day it is mixed for moulding the figures. The paste with the cornflour will ferment if not fresh, and will cause the figures to crack or distort.

For clothing or anything that requires rolling, use paste that has been stored for three to four days. Rework until pliable.

To store, wrap the paste in plastic and keep in a tightly covered container in the refrigerator. If the paste becomes hard and loses its elasticity, add water – drop by drop – until it is pliable again.

Pastillage

Pastillage is used for structural work, as it is stronger than paste. It has no elasticity, however, and does not allow much working time before setting. Pastillage pieces must be allowed to dry completely before continuing to work with them. They tend to warp while drying, so should be turned over every day during the drying period. When ready for use all edges must be sanded for neatness. An emery board is ideal for this purpose.

Pastillage No. 1
Pastillage No. 1 is strong and suitable for structural work, animals and bases. The disadvantage is that it sets very quickly, leaving a somewhat rough surface. If used for walls, it will need to be sanded smooth with an emery board or sand paper.

250 ml   (1 cup)   cold water
15 ml   (3 teaspoons)   gelatine
250 ml   (1 cup)   granulated sugar
1 kg   (± 2 lbs 2 oz)   sifted icing sugar

Pour half the water into a bowl and sprinkle the gelatine over it. Leave to sponge. Do not stir.

Put the granulated sugar into a pot and pour

5

over the rest of the water. Allow the sugar to dissolve slowly over low heat. Bring to the boil. *Do not stir.* Allow to boil until it reaches a temperature of 105° C (220° F) on a sugar thermometer, or until it makes a 2,5 cm-long (1 in.) thread when pulled between the fingers. To test, scoop up syrup on a wooden spoon, dip the fingers into *cold* water, take a drop of syrup between the fingers and pull the fingers apart. If a syrup thread of 2,5 cm (1 in.) can be made, the mixture is ready. Remove from the heat.

Dissolve the sponged gelatine over boiling water. Add to the syrup as soon as it is removed from the stove and mix until the gelatine has dissolved completely. Stir in icing sugar (about 500 ml [2 cups]) until the mixture resembles heavy cream.

Store the pastillage in an airtight container. Refrigerate until required.   To use, take small amounts of pastillage at a time and knead in some of the remaining icing sugar until firm enough to mould.

Note If the gelatine is not completely dissolved, it will cause dark specks in the pastillage.

Pastillage No. 2

Pastillage No. 2 does not set as quickly as Pastillage No. 1 and allows a little more working time for modelling. It also has a smoother finish. It is suitable for making bases for figures, animals and furniture. The disadvantage is that it is not as strong as Pastillage No. 1 when used for structural work. It also takes longer to dry.

250 ml	(1 cup)	cornflour
250 ml	(1 cup)	sifted pure icing sugar
15 ml	(3 teaspoons)	gelatine
80 ml	($\frac{1}{3}$ cup) cold	water
10 ml	(2 teaspoons)	liquid glucose
5 ml	(1 teaspoon)	cream of tartar

Sift the cornflour and icing sugar together. Sprinkle the gelatine over the cold water and leave to soak until spongy. Heat the glucose until melted and remove from the heat. Add the sponged gelatine and cream of tartar. Stir until completely dissolved. Make a well in the cornflour and sugar mixture, add the hot liquid and stir to blend gradually. Mix well. The mixture will have the consistency of heavy whipped cream. Store in an airtight container.

Take small amounts of the mixture at a time and knead in additional icing sugar until the consistency is firm enough for moulding or rolling out.

Rolling and cutting out pastillage

Trace the required pattern pieces onto light cardboard. Cut them out. Tint the pastillage by kneading in the required colouring. Light colours can be used immediately, but dark colours should be allowed to stand for a few minutes before rolling out.

Dust the rolling surface (preferably marble or smooth Formica) with cornflour. Place spacers of the right thickness on either side to ensure uniformity. Roll the pastillage to the exact thickness required. Don't turn the pastillage over while rolling, but lift it from time to time to dust the rolling surface with a little cornflour to prevent sticking. Cut off a piece of pastillage and compare it with the thickness chart below.

To cut out, position the largest templates on the pastillage first. Always use a sharp knife. If the pastillage is thick, wet the point of the blade and cut slowly and carefully to obtain a sharp edge. If there are windows or other openings, cut them out first while carefully holding down the template. Remove the areas that have been cut out. Cut out the outer edges, cutting away from the corners and not towards them.

Cut smaller pattern pieces from the remaining rolled-out pastillage. To avoid distortion, place a piece of pastillage slightly larger than the pattern piece on glass. Position the pattern piece on top and cut out. Remove the edges and leave the pastillage pattern piece on the glass until dry.

To avoid warping, dry the pattern pieces on glass dusted with cornflour. Leave for half a day, place another piece of glass on top and turn over carefully. Remove the original glass. Repeat until completely dry.

Thickness chart for pastillage

For best results the thickness of the pastillage should be matched to the size of the article being modelled. For example, the walls of a house should be thicker than the furniture. The following thicknesses were used for the projects in this book.

— Fine (1 mm [$\frac{1}{25}$ in.]) – used for cards and plaques

▬ Standard (2 mm [$\frac{2}{25}$ in.]) – used for furniture, e.g. chest of drawers

▬ Medium (3 mm [$\frac{3}{25}$ in.]) – used for chairs and church on wedding cake

▬ Semi-thick (4 mm [$\frac{4}{25}$ in.]) – used for tables

▬ Thick (5 mm [$\frac{1}{5}$ in.]) – used for walls and show boat

Note "Very thin" paste is sometimes specified for the projects in this book. This means almost transparent paste, to be used for clothing, ribbons, etc.

Gum glue

Gum glue is used to glue together the parts of the dolls and to attach the clothing when dressing the figures. It can also be used as a glaze.

1 part gum arabic (acacia)
3 parts cold water
drop of rose water

Place the ingredients in a screw-top jar. Shake well. Store in the refrigerator.

Royal icing

Royal icing is made from egg white and sifted icing sugar. For best results it should be beaten by hand and not in a food mixer. It is used mainly for making the hair of the figures and for tube flowers, flood work and finishing off the sides of cakes with embroidery, lacework and filigree. As it is strong, it is also used to glue together pieces of pastillage structures. *Note* Do not use reconstituted egg white to join pastillage pieces, as it does not adhere properly.

1 egg white, at room temperature
$\pm$ 200 g ($\pm$ 6 $\frac{1}{2}$ oz) icing sugar

Strain the egg white through a dry muslin cloth (this will break up the egg white while retaining its thickening effect). Beat lightly by hand.

Sift the icing sugar through a very fine sieve, nylon stocking, a piece of organdy or similar material. Add to the egg white gradually and mix to a soft, creamy consistency. Add just enough icing sugar so that a sharp and smooth peak forms and holds when the spoon is lifted out of the mixture. If the icing mixture is too soft, the peak will droop. If too much icing sugar has been used, the peak will break off.

If too stiff, dip a spatula holding a small quantity of icing mixture into beaten egg white and mix this into the rest of the icing mixture. Repeat the process until the correct consistency is reached. (This method ensures that you will not end up with an enormous bowl of mixed icing.)

Royal icing will be snow white if it has been mixed correctly. To make it even brighter, dip the tip of the handle of a brush into blue colouring and mix this trace into the icing. If not well mixed, the royal icing will be slightly creamy in colour.

Sugar rocks

Sugar rocks are used for garden scenes.

1 kg (2 lbs 2 oz) granulated sugar
250 ml (1 cup) cold water
$\frac{1}{2}$ recipe royal icing (see above), well beaten to incorporate as much air as possible

Melt the sugar in the water over a low temperature, then boil to 130° C (280° F) as measured on a sugar thermometer. Remove from the stove. Immediately stir in the well-beaten royal icing. Pour into a shoe box or similar container lined with well-greased wax paper. The mixture will bubble up to double its original volume. Leave to cool, then break up into rocks of the required sizes.

If coloured rocks are required, colour the royal icing beforehand. To make sand and gravel, crush pieces of sugar rock with a rolling pin.

Modelling techniques

Modelling human figures

Proportions
To ensure that the figures are lifelike, certain proportions have to be followed. These proportions differ for men and women, and for children according to their age. The head is taken as the basic measurement (see *fig. 1*):
- An adult man is 7,5-8 heads tall
- An adult woman is 6,5-7 heads tall

Fig. 1
The proportions of men, women and children with the head taken as the basic measurement.

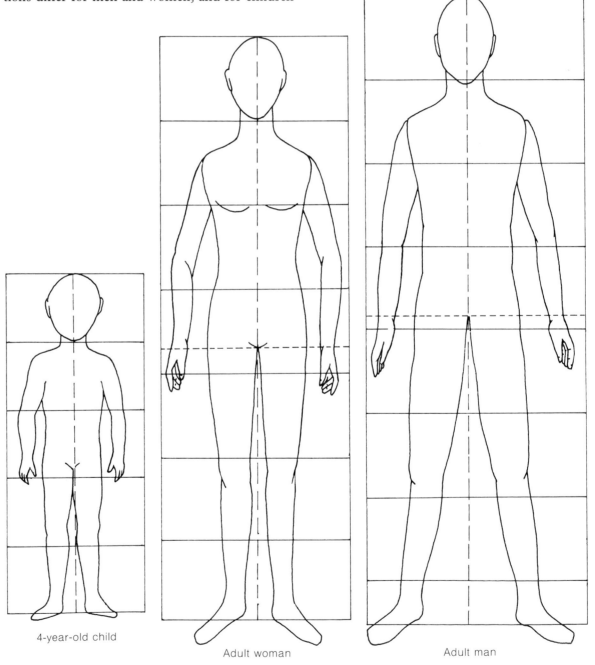

4-year-old child

Adult woman

Adult man

- A 1-year-old child is 4 heads tall
- A 4-year-old child is 5 heads tall
- A 9-year-old child is 6 heads tall

For the proportions of the arms and hands, see Modelling arms and hands, p. 12.

Colouring the skin

Paste used for skin should be coloured before the figures are modelled. Add flesh-tinted vegetable colouring to the paste until the correct skin tone has been obtained. Make the colour slightly darker than desired, as the paste will become lighter as it dries.

Be careful not to make the skin tone too pink or too yellow. To correct pinkness, add yellow; vice versa if the skin is too yellow.

For a black skin, start with a light flesh-coloured paste and add brown until the colour is as dark as desired. Add green to obtain the correct skin tone.

For an Indian skin, add less brown than for a black skin and add blue instead of green.

For a Japanese or Chinese skin, add yellow and green to a light skin tone.

Modelling the figure of a woman

Making a 185 mm-tall (7 $\frac{2}{5}$ in.) female figure
To make the base of the body, model a piece of pastillage 95 mm (3 $\frac{4}{5}$ in.) long with a diameter of 30 mm (1 $\frac{1}{5}$ in.) at the top and slightly wider at the bottom (see *fig. 2a*). Insert a 180 mm (7 $\frac{1}{5}$ in.) wooden skewer lengthways into the centre of the base with the point downwards. Leave to dry.

To shape the head and torso, roll a sausage of skin-coloured paste. Rub the surface until satin smooth and free of any cracks. Dust lightly with cornflour. (Never dust the mould with cornflour, as it will clog the facial features.) Press the paste into the mould for the back of the figure and trim off any excess paste (see *fig. 2b*). Use a skewer to make a slot in the centre to accommodate the skewer protruding from the base (see *fig. 2c*). Remove from the mould, rest on a flat surface and cover with cling film if the atmosphere is hot and dry.

Cast the front as the back. Press the paste firmly into the mould to ensure the facial features will be formed. View the mould from the side to see whether the nose and chin are pressed completely into the mould. Remove.

Apply gum glue to the back of the figure and the skewer. Press the back onto the skewer (see *fig. 2c*). Push the front and the back together, making sure the edges are well joined. Remove any excess glue and rub the joins smooth.

Hold an index finger under the chin while assembling the figure to prevent wrinkles from

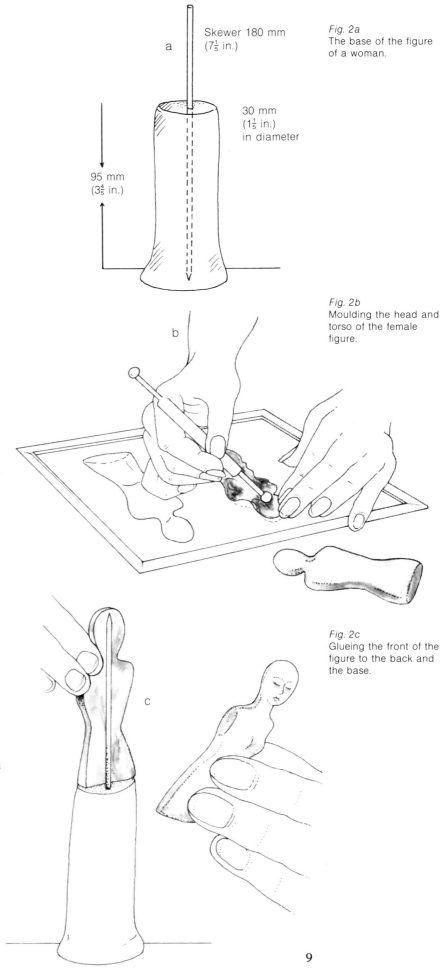

Skewer 180 mm (7$\frac{1}{5}$ in.)

30 mm (1$\frac{1}{5}$ in.) in diameter

95 mm (3$\frac{4}{5}$ in.)

Fig. 2a
The base of the figure of a woman.

Fig. 2b
Moulding the head and torso of the female figure.

Fig. 2c
Glueing the front of the figure to the back and the base.

9

forming while the paste is still pliable (see *fig. 2d*). Still supporting the chin, set the head at the desired angle. Push 24-gauge wire through the seams at shoulder level where the arms will be attached (see *fig. 2d*). Leave the figure to dry.

For a sitting figure, use a shorter skewer for the torso and a piece of 18-gauge wire for the legs (see *fig. 2e* and *2f*).

Modelling the figure of a man
Making a 200 mm-tall (8 in.) male figure
Use pastillage No. 1 or No. 2 as required for the legs. Roll into a sausage shape about 120 mm (4 $\frac{4}{5}$ in.) long and about 30 mm (1 $\frac{1}{5}$ in.) in diameter.

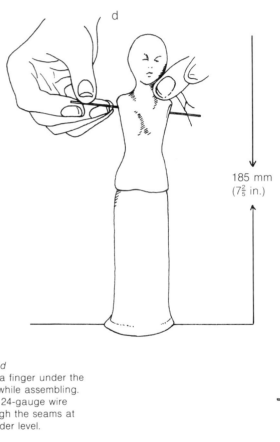

185 mm
(7 $\frac{2}{5}$ in.)

Fig. 2d
Hold a finger under the chin while assembling. Push 24-gauge wire through the seams at shoulder level.

Fig. 2e
Sitting figure.

Fig. 2f
Sitting figure.

Cut the two ends straight across to obtain neat edges. Flatten the sausage slightly. Dip two wooden skewers into gum glue and push into the sausage, sharp ends upwards, at a slight angle so that they protrude from the top end of the sausage (see *fig. 3*). The bottom of the skewers should not be too close to either the inside or the outside of the sausage, but in the centre of the two legs to be formed. Leave about 20 mm ($\frac{4}{5}$ in.) of the skewers protruding from the bottom of the sausage.

To form the legs, cut an inverted V about 90 mm (3 $\frac{3}{5}$ in.) long between the two skewers. Remove the excess pastillage. To prevent the back of the legs from being flattened, the pastillage can be laid down on cotton wool. Shape the lower torso and each leg and heel, smoothing the inside where the pastillage was cut and ensuring that the legs are of equal size. The legs must be far enough apart for two trouser legs to fit between them. Stand the figure upright in a block of polystyrene to ensure that it is straight and not angled to one side.

Use paste to mould the front of the feet. The feet should be at least the length of the head and must be equal in size. The heels must be narrow and the feet should turn out slightly.

If the legs are to be bent, do not use skewers but 18-gauge wire and bend as desired. Prop up the figure and allow to dry thoroughly.

Mould the upper torso as for the figure of a woman (see p. 9). Model the arms and hands as described on p. 12.

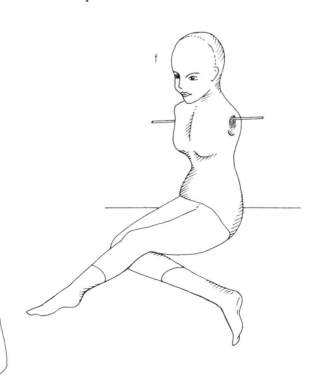

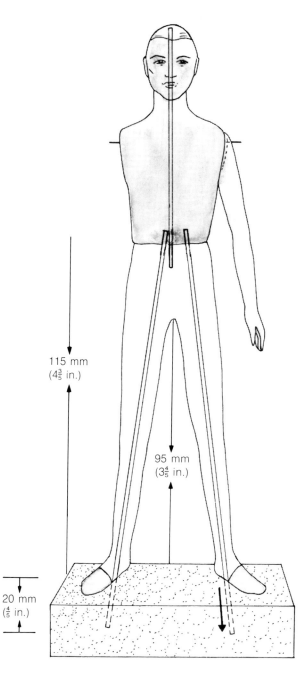

115 mm
(4⅗ in.)
95 mm
(3⅘ in.)
20 mm
(⅘ in.)

Fig. 3
Modelling the figure of a man.

Modelling the figure of a child

Press flesh-coloured paste into the head mould for a child and shape the back of the head by hand. Push a toothpick through the neck into the head, leaving 20 mm (⅘ in.) to protrude from the neck (see *fig. 4c*). Remove and leave to dry completely.

Using body paste, make a pear shape three times the length of the head. Using straight scissors, slit the pointed end to 1,5 times the length of the head (see *fig. 4a*).

Separate and shape the legs, placing the knees one head length from the feet (see *fig. 4b*). Shape the feet (see *fig. 4c*). If the legs are to be bent, push 22-gauge wire into each leg and bend as required. If loose legs are required, shape the legs and torso as indicated in *fig 4d* and attach with wire running through the torso (see *fig. 4e-f*).

Push a piece of 24-gauge wire through the top of the body from shoulder to shoulder where the arms will be attached. Model the arms (see below).

Attach the head to the body by pushing the toothpick into the torso (see *fig. 4c*).

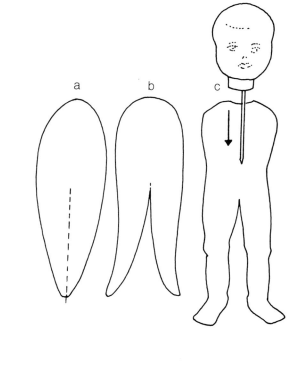

a
b
c
d
e
f

Fig. 4
Modelling the figure of a child.

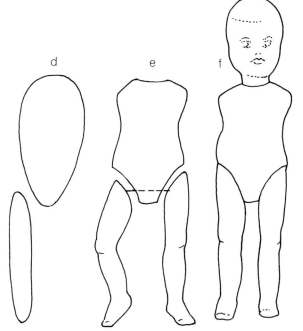

Modelling arms and hands

Find the length of the arms of men, women and children by measuring from the top of the shoulder to the waist; this is the length from the top of the arm to the elbow, and also from the elbow to the wrist, with the wrist level with the end of the torso.

Take two identical marble-sized pieces of paste and roll into sausage shapes. Form into an arm shape and flatten one end into a paddle shape (see *fig. 5a*), where the fingers will be formed.

To find the length of the hand, place the heel of the palm against the tip of the chin. The middle finger should reach the middle of the forehead (see *fig. 6*).

Using small, straight scissors, cut out a V on one side of the paddle to form the thumb (see *fig. 5b*). Make three more cuts, level with the top third of the thumb, to form the fingers (see *fig. 5c*). Dampen your fingers on a wet cloth or rub fat on your hands. Working very carefully, separate the figure's fingers slightly and gently shape with a back-and-forth movement (see *fig. 5d*). Make the nails. With the back of a scalpel, make the finger joints (see *fig. 5e*). Use the handle of the scalpel to make the wrist. Bend the thumb towards the palm (see *fig. 5f*).

Shape the top of the arm by cutting it at an angle using straight scissors (see *fig. 5g*). Carefully position the arm at the shoulder by pushing it onto the wire that runs through the upper

Fig. 5
Modelling arms and hands.

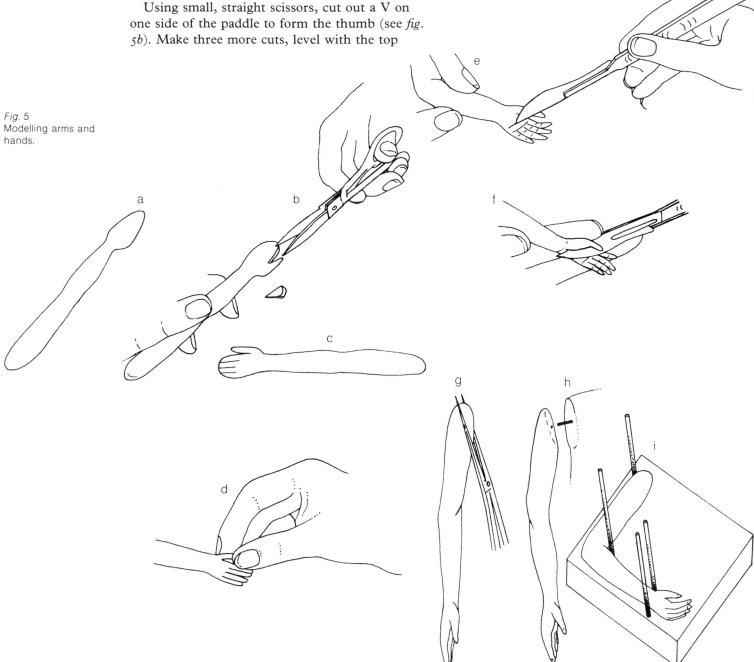

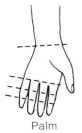 

Palm   Back of hand

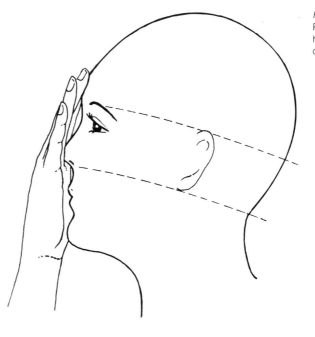

Fig. 6
Proportions of the
hand and the position
of the ear.

torso (see *fig. 5h*). When the arm is in the correct position, remove it from the wire and leave to set. To ensure that the arm dries correctly, it can be held in place with toothpicks pushed into polystyrene (see *fig. 5i*).

Hints
■ From the wrist to the elbow and the elbow to the shoulder the arm has straight bones and should not be allowed to bend.
■ The back of the hand must be flat.
■ Remember to make a left and a right arm and hand.
■ Women's hands should taper gracefully. The nails can be manicured by dipping a small brush into gum glue followed by pink colouring. Just touch the tips of the fingers to indicate nails.
■ Men's hands are slightly broader than those of women and the fingers have blunter ends.
■ Children's hands are short and plump.
■ The curve of the hand differs for men, women and children.
■ In a relaxed position a man's hand forms an open fist.
■ For a woman's hand the middle and ring fingers are together and slightly curled, while the index and little fingers are curled less and slightly higher than the other two fingers.
■ A child's hand forms a loose fist.

Modelling ears
Roll a piece of paste the size of a pinhead into a very thin sausage. Make the lower end slightly thicker and bend it into the shape of a C. Position the ear on the side of the head just in front of the join (see *fig. 7*). The tip of the ear should be in line with the eyebrow and the earlobe in line with the tip of the nose (see *fig. 6*).

Make-up

MAKE-UP FOR ADULTS
The figures must be allowed to dry thoroughly before the make-up is applied. Do this before the figures are dressed. Mistakes can be removed with a razor blade or a scalpel, but be careful not to damage the facial features.

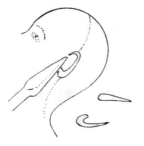

Fig. 7
Modelling the ears.

Eyes
Use a sharp 3H pencil to draw the crease above the upper eyelid from the inside corner to the centre (see *fig. 8a*). Draw a line for the lower eyelid from corner to corner. Fill in the white of the eye with a white pencil, drawing a small circle for the iris. Part of the top of the iris should be concealed by the top eyelid. Decide how the light is going to strike the eye and ensure it is the same for both eyes. Colour in the iris, leaving a white light spot. Draw a black pupil in the centre of the eye. Draw the lower line of the top eyelid from the inner to the outer corner, extending with an upward sweep for the eyelash (see *fig. 8b* for a correct and *fig. 8c* for an incorrect eye).

Continue drawing in the lashes towards the centre of the eye, making each stroke shorter than the previous one. Stop at the centre of the eye. Using a fine pink food pen make a small dot at the inner corner of the eye to mark the tear duct – this is very important, as it makes the eye come alive.

13

Fig. 8a
Applying make-up.

Fig. 8b
Correct eye.

Fig. 8c
Incorrect eye.

Fig. 8d
Correct mouth shape.

Fig. 8e
Incorrect mouth shape.

Fig. 8f
Ageing the face.

Fig. 8g
Making up children.

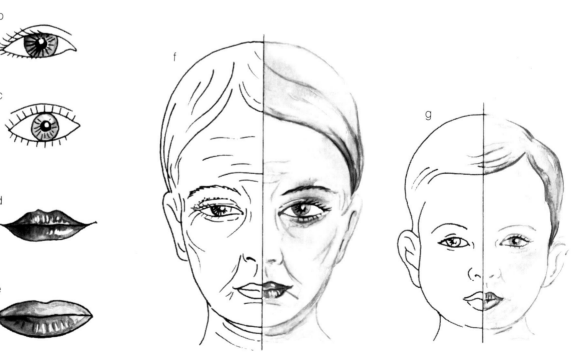

Using light grey dusting powder, shade the inner nose in line with the eye. A light dusting of eyeshadow can be applied to the outer eyelids. Feather the eyebrows using a pencil to match the hair colour.

Nose
Lightly indicate the nostrils using a very fine, sharp grey pencil. Start at the inner corner of the nostril, making a dot, then continue into a curve (see *fig. 8a*).

Mouth
With a 3H pencil draw a faint line between the upper and lower lips from one corner of the mouth to the other. Fill in the lips with a pink pencil or lipstick applied with a very fine brush. Don't take the colour to the corner of the mouth (see *fig. 8d* for the correct shape and *fig. 8e* for the wrong shape). For a man or child, use a light pink shade instead of deep pink or red – don't omit the lip colour, as it helps to define the mouth.

Blusher
Starting in line with the centre of the eye, apply blusher or pink dusting powder and brush it up to the temple. Fill in below this shading (see *fig. 8a*). Dust the chin, tip of the nose and centre of the forehead with blusher.

Ageing
Ageing can be achieved by following *fig. 8f*. Mark the wrinkles on the face with a veining tool as soon as the two halves of the head have been joined and while the paste is still wet.

MAKE-UP FOR CHILDREN
To make up the faces of children, follow *fig. 8g*.

Hints
■ The eyelashes must slant and curve upwards.
■ The iris must be slightly masked by the top and/or bottom eyelid, otherwise the expression will suggest surprise or fear.
■ The lip colour must never extend to the corners (this will look messy and unnatural). Study your own mouth shape in a mirror to see how the lip fades into shadow.
■ Pay attention to detail to ensure a natural look.

Dressing figures

Fashions of the 18th, 19th and early 20th centuries

Theatrical yet accurate dressing of figures is a feature of Mexican sugar modelling. The doll-like human figures should not only be lifelike but also be dressed in period style. For this reason some research into dress fashions will be necessary before embarking on the design for a particular scene.

Fashion through the ages is a fascinating subject. For the projects in this book we gathered as much background information as possible. In this short summary we deal only with the period from the 18th to the early 20th century, as it lends itself so well to Mexican sugar art. We also would like you to experience the pleasure of discovering for yourself the interesting characteristics of and influences on the fashion era of your choice. For example, the wide Victorian crinoline had to be swept back with the advent of passenger trains, as the ladies couldn't pass through the narrow compartment doors! Hence the return of the bustle.

WOMEN'S FASHIONS
In the 18th century the French excelled themselves in the field of fashion. The most distinctive feature of this period was the powdered wig, which reached ridiculous heights by mid-century. To balance this excessive hairstyle, the wide-skirted bustle was replaced by hooped skirts. These in turn were replaced by very wide panniers. Towards the end of that century the powdered wig disappeared, to be replaced by loose ringlets and wide-brimmed hats.

Early in the 19th century the hooped skirt was replaced by the Empire-line. Large, scooped bonnets were worn and hairstyles were simple. Gradually waistlines dropped and the heavily corseted crinoline was in vogue by the mid-century. Hats became smaller and hairstyles more elaborate. This fashion gradually developed into the straighter skirt and bustle with emphasis on the back of the skirt. From 1860 the skirt train was back in fashion.

At the turn of the century hats became bigger as bustles disappeared. Although the hourglass figure was still fashionable, it became more of an S-line when viewed from the side.

MEN'S FASHIONS
Early in the 18th century men wore knee breeches, covered by a very elaborate frock coat over a waistcoat, with a great deal of emphasis on wide cuffs and lapels. Gradually cuffs became

less conspicuous and collars higher. Towards the end of the century, the corners of coats were cut away diagonally. Waistcoats became shorter, ending at the waist. Men's fashions generally became more sombre.

By the early 19th century tight, long trousers and high boots made an appearance, followed by long trousers over shorter boots. Fashions for men did not change much until the end of the century, when pinched-in waists and frock coats were back in vogue. By the end of the century the traditional suit for men was well established.

Hair was worn very long and elaborately dressed in the 18th century. This developed into the powdered wig, which remained in fashion until hairstyles became more simple, generally tied at the back with a bow. By the end of the century hair was loosely curled. Early in the 19th century hair became shorter; beards and sideburns were becoming fashionable, and remained so into the 20th century.

The tricorne hat persisted throughout the 18th century with many variations, e.g. wide brims, plumes, etc. This gave way to cocked hats and by the end of the century the narrow-brimmed, high-crowned top hat emerged. Throughout the 19th century it saw many variations until the Homburg, bowler and boater hats as well as caps became common at the end of the 19th century.

Basic dressing of a female figure

Make up the face before dressing the figure (see p. 14).

To make a shoe, take a small piece of paste the size of a small pea and shape it into a pointed cone about 10 mm ($\frac{2}{5}$ in.) long. Using gum glue, attach the flat end slightly off centre to the front of the base of the figure to represent a shoe protruding from a long dress (see *fig. 19a*). Make only one shoe.

Attach a narrow Garrett frill around the base, lifting it over the shoe. (The frill will probably not be visible, but should a small section of the skirt lift up, the frilly petticoat will show and not the base of the figure.)

Trace the basic patterns for a woman's dress (see *pattern 1*, p. 67) onto thin cardboard and cut out. Roll out coloured paste for the garments until paper thin. Using the cardboard templates, cut out the skirt back using a sharp scalpel. Gather the top of the skirt to fit across the back of the waist. Apply gum glue across the back of the figure just below the waist and down both sides. Attach the skirt to the figure, allowing the paste to hang in natural folds.

Cut out the skirt front. Fold the sides under to form a loose pleat. Gather the skirt at the waist.

Apply gum glue across the front of the figure just below the waist and down both sides of the skirt back. Attach the skirt front to the figure by pressing gently on the glued area. Using a toothpick, press the top of the skirt against the waistline to ensure it is well secured and to mark out fine gathers.

Cut out the bodice back. Apply gum glue across the shoulders, around the back of the neck, around the armhole but not right up to the arm wire, down both sides and across the waist. Attach the dress back to the figure. By leaving the back free of gum glue the paste will stand away slightly from the body, creating a natural effect. The waistlines of the bodice and the skirt must just meet and not overlap, as this will thicken the waist.

Using half the basic front bodice pattern, cut out the left bodice front. Apply gum glue to the back shoulder line, around the front neckline, down the front, around the armhole, down the side and across the waistline. Attach the left front in position, making sure the side seams are straight.

Using the other half of the basic front pattern, cut out the right bodice front. Apply gum glue as for the left bodice front. Attach the right front in position. Mark the buttonholes. Roll pinhead-sized pieces of paste into balls and flatten to look like buttons. Lift each with a pin, touch with gum glue and position over the buttonholes.

Cut out the collar (see *Doll's wardrobe, pattern 5*, p. 70). Roll the neck edge under. Apply gum glue to the underside and attach to the neckline of the dress.

To make a sash, roll out a small piece of paste as thinly as possible. Cut out a strip to fit around the waist. Apply gum glue around the waistline of the figure, position the centre front of the sash at the centre front of the figure and bring the ends together at the back. Cut two more strips for the sash ends and attach with gum glue, allow the sash to hang down naturally at the back. Using the remaining pieces of paste, make a bow and place it over the joins at the back.

Dress the arms before attaching them to the figure. Cut out the sleeves. *Note* One side of the sleeve cap is wider than the other; the wider part should be at the back. Apply a line of gum glue down the centre of the inner arm to the wrist. Position the sleeve edge under the arm and wrap the sleeve around the arm. Apply gum glue to the attached edge, overlap the front edge and trim off any excess. The join must always face down. If the arm is in a bent position, make a small fold at the elbow.

Fold back the loose sleeve cap, position the

arm on the figure and cut off any wire that protrudes beyond the arm. Remove the arm and cover the hole on the outside of the arm with a very small piece of paste. Bring the sleeve cap back into position. Apply gum glue to the top edge of the arm. Make small tucks in the sleeve cap to fit the arm. Trim off any excess paste, leaving the inner hole in the arm free. Apply gum glue to the wire. Taking a small ball of paste, push it over the wire, pressing against the body. Apply more gum glue over the ball of paste. Apply gum glue to the inside top of the arm where it fits to the body. Press the arm into position. If necessary, prop up the arm with foam until set. Dress the other arm to be a mirror image of the first one and place in position.

Making the hair Colour royal icing as required. Fill a piping bag with the royal icing. Using a No. 1 tube, pipe the hairline along the forehead and cover the head with icing. Dip a finger into cornflour and firmly press the icing against the head (see *fig. 9a*) so that the hair seems to be growing out of the head. Build up the hairstyle

in front by adding more royal icing. Dip a scalpel into cornflour and mark to represent strands of hair (see *fig. 9b*). Repeat at the back of the head. If desired, make ringlets by roping (see *fig. 9c*) or copy any of the styles in *plate 2*.

If the figure will be wearing a hat, make the hat as described on p. 21. Push the hat onto the head after the hair styling has been completed and while the icing is still wet.

Basic dressing of a male figure
Make up the face before dressing the figure (see p. 14).

Apply glaze to the shoes. If the figure will be wearing spats, add them at this stage.

Trace the basic patterns for the man's clothing (see *pattern 2*, p. 68) onto thin cardboard and cut out. Roll paste out very thinly and cut out the trousers. Apply gum glue to the figure from the centre front and centre back of the waistline to the crotch and down the inner legs to the shoes. Starting at the centre back of the waistline, place the trousers in position (see *fig. 10a–b*). Fit the trousers firmly into the crotch and down the in-

Fig. 9
Making the hair of royal icing.

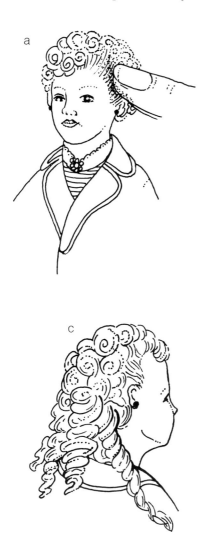

ner legs. Wrap each trouser leg round to the front and glue down the inner leg. If the knee is bent, make sure the paste folds like fabric would have done.

Cut out the shirt front. Apply gum glue around the front neckline, across the shoulders and down the chest of the figure. Place the shirt in position (see *fig. 10c*).

Cut out the shirt collar. Fold as indicated on the pattern. Apply gum glue around the neckline. Position the centre of the collar at the centre of the neckline, bringing both ends round to meet at the centre front.

Cut out the tie. Make a pleat at the top. Apply gum glue to the top and wrap the knot over. Place in position, lifting the corners of the collar if necessary (see *fig. 10c*).

Cut out the right side of the waistcoat and then the left (see dotted lines on pattern piece for jacket front). Overlap the right-hand side over the left (see *fig. 10d*). Mark the buttonholes and place the buttons in position. Add pocket flaps.

Cut out the jacket back. If a centre back vent or two side vents are required, mark them in at this stage. Apply gum glue around the neckline up to the shirt collar, across the back shoulders, around the arms and down both sides to below the waist, over the trousers and across the waist. Place the jacket back in position.

Cut out the right jacket front. Mark the pocket flap positions. Apply glue to the inside of the fold line, fold over the jacket revers and crease well (see *fig. 10d*). Apply glue to the shoulder up to the jacket back, ensuring that the seam is straight, around the armhole and down the side. Place in position, bringing the seams together to join exactly. Make and position the left front jacket to be a mirror image of the right side. Mark in the buttonholes.

Plate 2 (p. 18)
Elaborate hairstyles circa 1876. (From *Victorian fashions and costumes from Harper's Bazar 1867-1898*, edited by Stella Blum, Dover Publications, Inc., New York, 1974.)

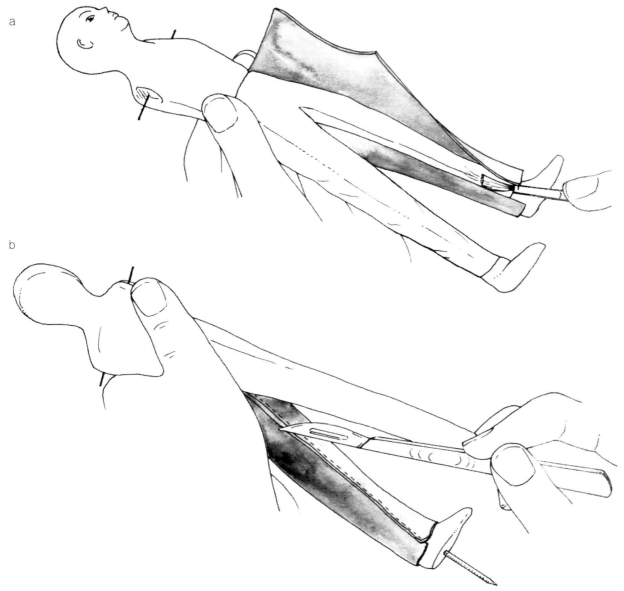

a

b

Fig. 10
Basic dressing of the figure of a man.

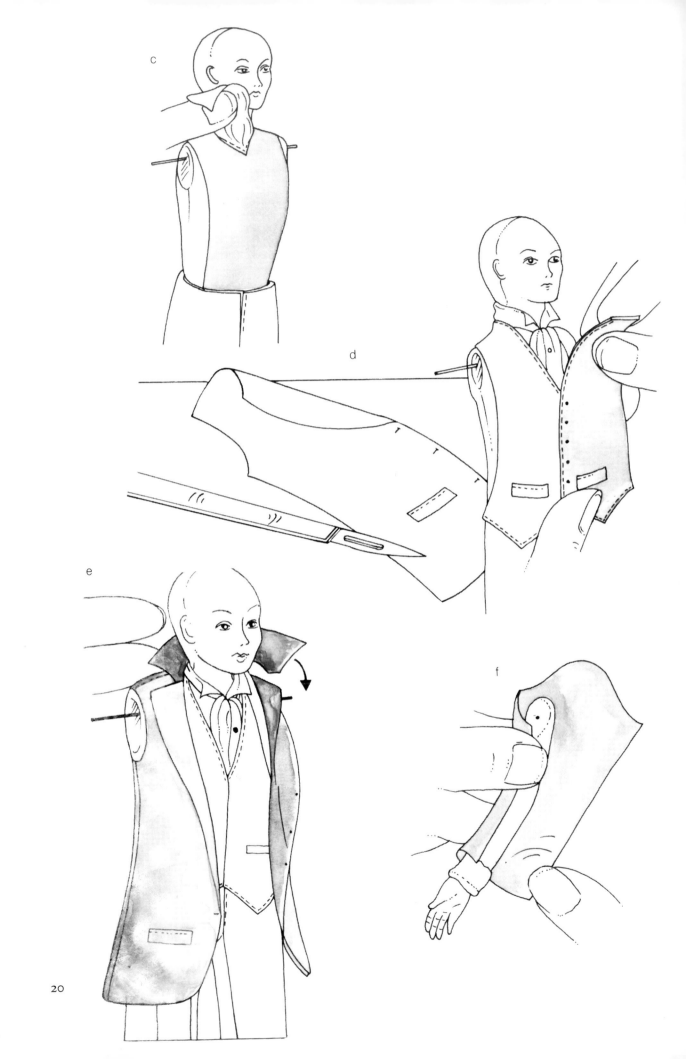

Cut out the jacket collar. Fold on the crease line. Apply gum glue to the edge of the collar (see *fig. 10e*). Place in position so that the collar just touches the front revers but does not overlap.

Place the pocket flaps in position and the buttons on the buttonholes.

Cut out a shirt cuff and glue to the wrist. Decorate with a cuff link. Cut out the right jacket sleeve. Apply gum glue down the inner arm. Position the back edge of the sleeve at the inner arm, wrapping the sleeve around the arm and overlapping the back seam (see *fig. 10f*). Rub the seam smooth with the back of a scalpel. Crease the sleeve at the elbow if the arm is bent.

Fold the top of the sleeve back, place the arm in position on the torso and cut off any wire that protrudes beyond the arm. Remove the arm. Cover the hole at the outside of the arm with a small piece of paste. Paint gum glue around the top edge of the arm, leaving the hole in the inner arm open. Fold the sleeve over the top of the arm, easing out the fullness so that there are no folds.

Apply gum glue to the wire and to the torso around the arm. Push a small ball of paste over the wire, pressing against the torso, and apply more gum glue over the paste. Apply gum glue to the inside of the arm over the sleeve, pressing the arm to the torso. Dress the other arm to be a mirror image of the first.

Hint Only the shirt front and cuffs are visible, so apply them only.

Making the hair Colour royal icing as required. Fill a piping bag with the royal icing. Using a No. 1 tube, pipe the hairline along the forehead and cover the head with icing. Dip a finger into cornflour and firmly press the royal icing against the head, bringing the sideburns down in front of the ears. Dip a scalpel into cornflour and mark to resemble strands of hair. Repeat at the back of the head.

If the figure will be wearing a hat, make it as described below. Push the hat onto the head after the hairstyle has been completed and while the hair of royal icing is still pliable.

Making the beard Use the same royal icing as for the hair. Start piping the moustache from above the centre of the upper lip and draw it outwards. Using a wet brush, blend the edges into the skin. Repeat for the other side.

Making the eyebrows Take a small dab of royal icing as for the hair, thin it down with water and paint it onto the brows with a very fine brush.

Basic dressing of the figure of a child

Trace the basic patterns for the child's clothing (see *pattern 3*, p. 69) onto thin cardboard and cut out. To dress the figure of a boy, follow the instructions for dressing the figure of a man (see p. 19-20). To dress the figure of a girl, follow the instructions for dressing the figure of a woman (see p. 16).

If stockings are worn, model the legs in the colour of the stockings and shape the shoes over the feet. If the dress is short, e.g. the *Three little girls* birthday cake (see *plate 14*, p. 48), the figure can also be dressed in knickers. Make the knickers following the child's trousers pattern, but cut the legs shorter.

Accessories

HATS

Make a bust of a male and a female figure to use as dummies when making hats. For examples of hats and trimmings, see *plates 3-4* and *plates 5-6*, p. 21-22.

Plate 3
Examples of hats, hairstyles, necklines and trimmings as seen from the front.

Plate 4
Examples of hats, hairstyles, necklines and trimmings as seen from the back.

Plate 5
Examples of hats, necklines and trimmings as seen from the front.

Plate 6
Examples of hats, necklines and trimmings as seen from the back.

Making women's hats

Model the crown of the hat to the desired shape on the dummy. If the hat has a brim, remove the crown, cut out the brim and place it on the dummy. Apply gum glue to the edge of the crown, press onto the brim and decorate as desired. Leave the hat on the dummy to set.

Making men's hats

Cut out the brim. Place in position on the head. Shape the crown and attach to the brim.

Hints

■ Do not allow gum glue to touch the dummy, as you will not be able to remove the hat when set.

■ Always place the hat on the figure while the hair is still pliable. The hair will then mould naturally into the hat. If the hair is allowed to dry first, the hat will no longer fit the head.

■ A top hat splays out slightly at the top, while a Cromwell-style hat tapers towards the top.

PARASOLS

Parasols were an integral part of the wardrobe of every lady of fashion. To make a parasol, cut off a piece of florist's wire as long as required for the completed parasol and cover it with florist's tape. Cut out a circle of paste as large as required, make a hole in the centre, and divide it into six or eight equal portions (see *plate 8*, p. 23). Place in a parasol mould or suitable hollow object to shape. When dry, paint gum glue over the hole. Place a small ball of paste over the hole and insert the wire parasol handle (it may have a hook or be left straight). Allow a little of the wire to protrude at the top. Ensure that the handle remains in the centre while setting. Trim the top of the parasol with a narrow frill when set. Trim the rest of the parasol as desired. If an open parasol is to have a frill, make the frill and attach it to the parasol just before it is positioned over the figure's shoulder (see *The conversation, plate 37*, p. 59). This will ensure that the frill will fall naturally.

MUFFS

Muffs were very popular and varied in size from very large to just big enough for two hands. To make a muff, roll a piece of paste into a small cylindrical shape (remember it must be big enough for both hands). When dry, decorate as required (see *plate 7*).

FANS

In previous centuries a lady's wardrobe was not complete without a fan. To make a fan, roll out paste very thinly. Cut out a circle. Cut the circle in half to obtain two fans. Make folds in the fan as required. Apply gum glue to the folds where required if the fan should be half or completely closed. For an open fan, mark the spines with a scalpel. Trim the centre of the base with a disc or ribbon. Decorate as required (see *plate 7*, p. 23).

TRIMMINGS

When making trimmings (see *plate 7*, p. 23), always roll out the paste as thinly as possible.

Making a bow

Roll out paste very thinly. Cut out two strips of the desired width and length for the loose ends. Glue one over the other at the top and cut each into the shape of a fork at the bottom. To make a looped knot, cut out a third strip of the same width but equal in length to the two ends together. Fold the short ends over to meet in the middle and glue together. Pinch in the centre to form folds and cover with a small strip of paste to form a knot. Attach the bow to the ribbons.

Make small rolls of wax paper and insert into the loops. Leave to set.

Making a feather
Cut a narrow teardrop shape out of paste. Point one end. Fold it in half lengthways to form a vein. Open out the feather again. Using a scalpel, cut fine lines on either side of the vein. To curl the feather, place it over a curved surface to dry.

Making ribbon roses
Cut out a thin strip of paste. Fold it in half lengthways and roll up like a bandage. Pinch the base to open out the rose. Glue a small circle of paste to the base. Trim with leaves cut from paste. Tiny roses made of royal icing can also be used for trimming.

Special effects
■ When dressing figures the paste must always be rolled out as thinly as possible for best results.
■ To make patterned fabric for dresses etc., roll out paste in the background colour. Roll out

paste in contrasting colour(s). Cut out flowers, stripes, dots or whatever pattern you wish to impose on the basic fabric. Be sure to use paper-thin paste. Place the coloured designs on the background paste. Dampen the contrasting paste with water if the air is dry. Roll out once more to blend the design into the background paste. Use as required to dress the figures.
■ To make self-embossed fabric, use leather embossers to create the design you want. Some lovely cake-decorating embossers have come onto the market recently.
■ To create a satin effect, dust the garment with pearl dust which is available in many beautiful shades.
■ To create a velvet look (see the man's jacket in *Show boat*, *plate 49*, p. 64) paint the garment with alcohol, e.g. gin, cane spirit or vodka. Take care, however, as the figure may become mouldy if kept for any length of time in damp conditions.
■ To obtain a textured corded look, roll the paste with a ridged bar obtainable from hardware stores. Many interesting effects can be achieved depending on the direction in which it is rolled and the size of the grooves of the ready bar. Experiment until the desired look is achieved.
■ To obtain accordion pleating, roll strips of paste with a ridged roller. Use for a woman's vest – it will give the appearance of faggotting, which was very popular in the 19th century (see the Edwardian figure seated on a bench in front of *The Victorian house*, *plate 50*, p. 65).
■ To create a lace effect, use a very fine length of ridged bar. Roll it diagonally one way. Use a No. O tube as a tool to make the open pattern of the lace, then roll the ridged bar diagonally in the opposite direction to open the pattern. For examples see the fans (*plate 7*, p. 23), the shawl in *Invitation to the dance* (*plate 35*, p. 58) and the frills on the bustle dress in *The conversation* (*plate 37*, p. 59).

Plate 7
Bows, ribbons and accessories.

Plate 8
Making parasols.

Modelling animals

When modelling animals, refer to art books or sculptures to obtain a good likeness and the illusion of movement. This is not easy but can be achieved with practice. In the case of horses in particular it is advisable to observe the animals closely. A good knowledge of the bone and muscle structure will be to your advantage. Otherwise work from a very clear picture or an artist's manual.

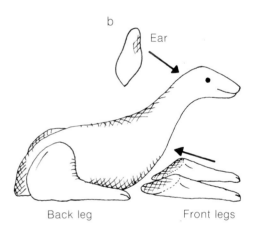

a

Torso

Back leg

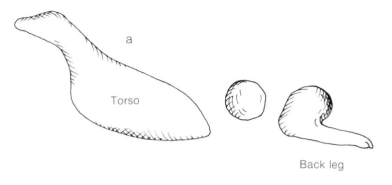

b

Ear

Back leg   Front legs

Modelling dogs

Dogs vary in shape and size and require close observation to obtain satisfactory results. Use pastillage No. 1 or No. 2 for the main part of the body, as it sets harder than paste. For the legs, ears, etc., paste should be used, as it allows more working time before setting.

To make the torso, model a pear-shaped piece of pastillage according to the size you require. Squeeze the narrow end with the fingers to form the snout (see *fig. 11a, left*). Using a toothpick, form the nostrils. Flatten the top of the snout. Mark the mouth with a scalpel. Using a small ball tool, mark the eye sockets. Roll the neck between the thumb and the index finger. Roll the chest and pinch in the flanks. Round off the buttocks.

To make the front legs, take two balls of paste of the same size (see *fig. 11a, centre*). Model with the fingers to shape the front legs (see *fig. 11b, right*).

To make the hind legs, take two larger pieces of paste (see *fig. 11a, right*). Bend the legs into the desired positions. Attach to the body with gum glue, supporting with pieces of polystyrene where necessary.

c

To make the ears, take two pieces of paste and shape as required (see *fig. 11b*). Attach to the head with gum glue.

To make the tail, roll a piece of paste as required and glue into position with gum glue. Leave the figure to dry.

When dry, place a small ball of white paste in each eye socket. Paint in the eyes, remembering to leave a white highlight in each eye. Outline the eyes with black pencil or paint. Paint the nose and mouth with food colouring.

Place the figure on wax paper. Using plain or coloured royal icing, pipe on the dog's coat (see *fig. 11c*). Use a flat paint brush to create the appearance of fur. If a long coat is required, bring the royal icing down onto the wax paper. Peel off the wax paper when dry.

If plain royal icing was used, paint the dog the appropriate colours when dry.

Modelling cats
Model cats in the same way as dogs. However, the nose should be shorter and the face much rounder and flatter (see the cat on the bench in *The Victorian house, plate 50*, p. 65).

To make whiskers, make pinpricks in the head to accommodate the whiskers. Push thin stamens into position when applying the coat of royal icing.

Modelling horses
Before starting, refer to an artist's manual or very clear photographs to get the right shape, proportions and movement. When modelling horses or other large animals, a wire armature will be necessary to support the weight. The inside of the horse remains hollow.

Make the wire armature (see *fig. 12a*). Let the wire protrude beyond the body for the tail.

Using pastillage No. 2, shape the skull. Using a small ball tool, make hollows for the ears. Model the nostrils. Place the skull in position on the wire armature, moulding the neck (see *fig. 12b*). Leave to dry.

Roll out pastillage No. 2 until 2 mm ($\frac{2}{25}$ in.) thick. Place over the wire armature "skeleton" to form a base on which to build the muscles. All joins should be situated under the body. Smooth any cracks on the outside by rubbing with a wet finger. Allow the first layer to set. When dry, add pastillage No. 2 where required to build up the muscles and skin.

Shape the ears as required and position over the ear hollows.

When the body is complete, add the tail and make the mane using royal icing. Paint and shade the horse as desired (see *Clydesdale horses, plate*

33, p. 57). When dry, paint with two or more coats of confectioner's glaze (available commercially) to obtain a shiny coat.

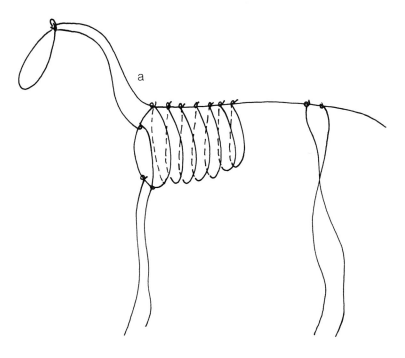

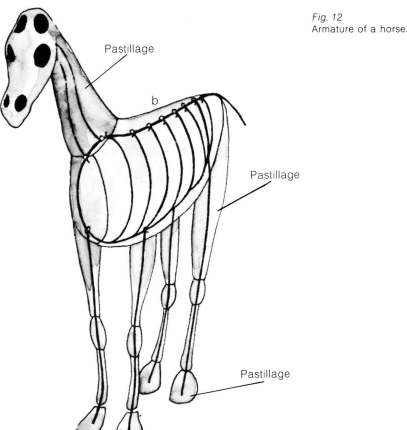

Fig. 12
Armature of a horse.

25

Structural work

Structural work is a fascinating aspect of Mexican modelling which opens up all sorts of opportunities for sugar craft. *The wedding* (*plates 22-25*, p. 51), *Show boat* (*plate 49*, p. 64), *The doll maker* (*plates 42-48*, pp. 62-63) and *The Victorian house* (*plates 50-54*, pp. 65-66) are different examples of this interesting technique.

Pastillage is always used for structural work, as it is much stronger than modelling paste. The two recipes given on pp. 5-6 have been used throughout this book. Where a great deal of weight and stress is put on the structures, e.g. *The Victorian house*, pastillage No. 1 should be used. For *The wedding*, where strength was less important than a smooth surface for the gazebo, pastillage No. 2 was used.

When designing a structure, draw all the templates accurately. Remember to allow for the thickness of the walls in your calculations. (Make the whole structure out of thin cardboard first to see whether it is the size you want. It is very deceptive to judge the size from the flat paper patterns.) Once the structure is standing you will have a much better idea of the finished size and will be able to make the necessary adjustments. If the walls are joined at a corner, a better fit is achieved by chamfering the ends of the wall. This should be done while the wall is soft – if further adjustments are required, the walls can be sanded when dry.

When rolling out the pastillage, use spacers of the required thickness to ensure that all pieces are of the same thickness (see p. 6).

Use royal icing made with fresh egg white to join the structural parts. It is much stronger than gum glue and ensures far better bonding. It is not necessary to use a tube in the icing bag, as the metal could hit the structure and break it. Be very generous when applying the royal icing. Bring the two parts of the structure together and smooth the inside of the work with a finger tip to force the icing into all the crevices. Clean the front of the work while the icing is still wet. If the structure does not have enough space for your hand, use a modelling tool to smooth the inside.

Polystyrene covered with wax paper can be propped up against the walls while they are drying to hold them in position. The wax paper peels off easily if it comes into contact with the icing. Books placed on the other side of the polystyrene will prevent any movement. Should any excess icing show on the front of the completed work, gently scrape off with a scalpel.

Stencilling

Stencilling is a very effective method of decorating walls such as in *The doll maker* (see *plate 42*, p. 62) and *The Christening cake* (see *plate 10*, p. 45). Many beautiful stencils are available on the market, but you may prefer to use your own design.

To make a stencil, take a 100 micron plastic sheet (available from art shops). Place the pattern you wish to copy under the plastic sheet and cut it out with a sharp scalpel (see *pattern 4*, p. 69). Thin cardboard can also be used to make a stencil. Draw the pattern onto the cardboard and cut out. The advantages of plastic are that it is easy to clean, will last longer and is more pliable than cardboard.

Position the stencil on the area you wish to decorate, making sure the stencil is secure (ask someone to hold it in place or tape it into position with masking tape). Spread royal icing in the colour required over the stencil and remove carefully for a raised design, or use dusting powders.

Cakes for special occasions

Christening cake

Plate 10

Prepare and cover a square cake measuring 300 m x 300 mm (12 in. x 12 in.), cutting away the corners. Cut a strip of paste 20 mm ($\frac{4}{5}$ in.) wide in a colour that contrasts with the background. Place the strip one quarter of the way down from the top to rest across the cake, down the sides and onto the board. Allow to dry for a few days before doing the stencilling. Place the stencil (see *pattern 4*, p. 69) on the strip and spread grey royal icing over the stencil. Lift it

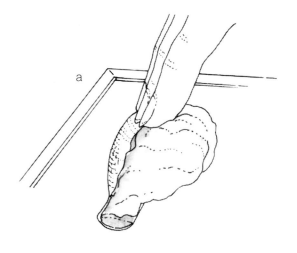

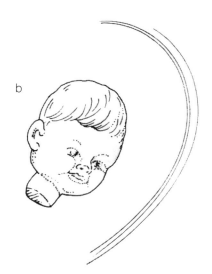

immediately, taking care not to smudge the wet icing.

Make the baby's face using a suitable mould. Press a small ball of paste into the mould with the right side facing you slightly higher than the mould (see *fig. 13a*) and the left side lower so that it slants. When released the face will be turned towards the right (see *fig. 13b*). Apply make-up and hair.

Using pastillage, make an oval plaque measuring 70 mm x 90 mm (2 $\frac{4}{5}$ in. x 3 $\frac{3}{5}$ in.). Attach the face of the baby to the plaque with royal icing. Dress the figure of the baby. Decorate the lower edge of the plaque with tiny royal-icing roses and leaves. Place the plaque in position on the cake. Decorate the cake with roses, maiden-hair ferns, ivy leaves and a ribbon made of paste.

To make the ribbon, roll the paste paper thin. Using a pastry wheel, cut out a 10 mm ($\frac{2}{5}$ in.) wide ribbon. Use an embossing tool to make the pattern. Dust with pink pearl dust.

Doll's wardrobe

Plate 11

Prepare and cover a rectangular cake measuring 360 mm x 280 mm (14 $\frac{2}{5}$ in. x 11 $\frac{1}{5}$ in.).

Using a suitable mould, model the doll entirely of paste. Model the arms and hands (see p. 12). Leave to dry completely for 3 to 4 days, depending on the weather. Dress her in a bathing costume.

Trace the clothing patterns (see *pattern 5*, p. 70) onto thin cardboard and cut out. Make up your own pattern for the evening dress in the lower left-hand corner.

Colour the paste before cutting out the garments. The paste may be patterned if desired (see Special effects, p. 23). Roll the paste out very thinly ($\pm$ 1 mm [$\frac{1}{25}$ in.]). Assemble the patterns into garments. Arrange the garments around the doll on the cake. Do not glue down the decorations; this will ensure they can be removed easily before the cake is cut.

Outline the top edges of the cake with anglaise

Fig. 13
Moulding the face for the christening cake.

lacework for a delicate finish and trim the sides with narrow multicoloured paste ribbons.

The magician

Plate 12

Prepare and cover a square cake measuring 260 mm x 260 mm (10 ⅖ in. x 10 ⅖ in.) with chamfered corners.

Using a suitable mould, mould the magician's body from paste and his legs from pastillage (see Modelling the figure of a man, p. 10). Allow to dry completely before dressing the figure (see Basic dressing of a male figure, pp. 19-20).

Make the table using pastillage. Model the rabbit (see Modelling animal figures, p. 24) and place into position. Roll paste out very thinly to resemble a cloth and cover the table, draping the cloth over the back of the rabbit.

Using coloured paste, make a jug, cards, balls, a hat, scarves and a length of rope. Allow to dry, then place into position. Decorate the corners of the cake with large and small stars in black and grey.

Prepare the two doves and a perch. To make each dove, prepare an armature by twisting together three strands of very thin white taped wire. Fold the wire over in half, make three twists in the centre for the body and fold the open ends down for the claws. Using paste, model the body and tail over the twists. Using a scalpel, mark out the feathers on the tail. When set, make the wings, mark the wing feathers and attach to the body with gum glue. Leave to dry. When dry, coat the whole bird with very soft white royal icing. Paint the eyes black. Pipe on a small beak. Repeat with the other dove.

Make a perch out of white taped wire. Open the three strands of wire that constitute the claws of the doves, bringing two strands forward and taking one back. Wrap the wires around the perch to support the doves.

Miss Muffet

Plate 13

Prepare and cover a round cake measuring 300 mm (12 in.) in diameter.

Using an appropriate mould, mould the body of Miss Muffet using paste. Make the legs of pastillage (see p. 10). One leg should be straight and attached to the flat ground with a skewer, while the other foot is on the grassy knoll with

the leg bent slightly. Place a 20-gauge wire in the leg that will be attached to the raised ground. Allow to dry completely before dressing each leg. Attach the legs to the torso.

Make up the face (see Make-up, p. 14), allowing the full circle of the iris to show to suggest a frightened look. Part the lips and pipe white royal icing in the mouth opening to form teeth.

Dress Miss Muffet (see Basic dressing of the female figure, p. 16). Before draping the skirt, place the left arm in position and catch the skirt in the hand. Allow to set. Remove the arm and dress before placing it in position permanently. Model the bowl and leave to dry. When modelling the right hand, bend the fingers around the bowl at an angle and leave to set.

Make the spider's legs from four strands of 32-gauge wire (see *fig. 14a*). Twist the wires together in the centre, then part them again to form eight legs, of which one should be raised. Using pastillage, model the spider's body over the centre twists. Using paste, make the spider's head and attach it to the body with gum glue (see *fig. 14b*). Model a small hat and glue it to the raised leg.

Pipe royal icing into the bowl to resemble curds and whey. Model a spoon.

Create a garden with modelled rocks (see Sugar rocks, p. 7), mushrooms, flowers, etc. Paint a scene around the side of the cake. Decorate the board as desired.

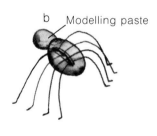

b Modelling paste

Three little girls

Plates 14-18

Prepare and cover a hexagonal cake, each side measuring 185 mm (± 7½ in.). The sides of the cake must be high enough (± 110 mm [± 4½ in.]) to accommodate the side pictures.

Model the three little girls (see Modelling the figure of a child, p. 11). Make and attach the legs in the correct positions (see *plate 14*, p. 48). Strengthen the legs attached to the cake with a toothpick, as the bodies are supported by only one leg each. Model the arms and the hands (see

Fig. 14
Making the spider.

Modelling arms and hands, p. 12) in the correct positions to hold the banner.

Apply make-up. Dress the figures using the basic child's clothing patterns (see *pattern 3*, p. 69).

Make the balloons by hollowing a circle of paste into a half round using a ball tool. When set, make another the same way. Set thin taped wire into one half round and glue it to the other half with gum glue. (The balloons must be hollow, otherwise they will be too heavy to be supported by the wire.) For the balloons on the side of the cake, use only one half.

Model the cat (see Modelling animal figures, p. 24). Using royal icing, attach the cat to the cake. When complete, attach the balloons to the ribbon around the neck of the cat.

Decorate the side of the cake with pictures of party games. On this particular cake one little girl carries a cake, one opens gifts and one pins a tail on a picture of a donkey. To make the side pictures, use the bas-relief technique (see Bas-relief work, *The Kate Venter Sugar Art Collection*, p. 21). Trace *pattern 6*, p. 71 on paper, put under clear plastic and model the figures over this. Attach to the side of the cake using royal icing.

To make the banner, roll out paste very thinly. Cut to the correct size. Leave to dry. Pipe on the lettering "Happy Birthday" and trim with picot edging. Set the wire posts in position and allow to dry completely. To attach the posts to the girls' hands, pipe icing into each hand and push in the posts (it may be necessary to support the posts until dry).

The rugby player

Plate 19

Prepare and cover a rectangular cake measuring 320 mm x 230 mm (12 in. x 9 in.).

Using an appropriate mould, model the entire figure of the rugby player from paste. Make the legs separately, inserting wire into the bent leg. Allow to set. Add the socks and shoes before attaching each leg to the torso using royal icing.

Allow to dry completely before dressing the figure (see Basic dressing of a male figure, p. 17). To make the striped jersey, see Special effects, p. 23.

Decorate each corner of the cake with a rosette. To make a rosette, roll out paste very thinly into a strip measuring 30 mm x 1 mm (1 $\frac{1}{5}$ in. x $\frac{1}{25}$ in.). Pleat into a circle. Roll out another strip in the second colour to measure 30 mm x 2 mm

(1 $\frac{1}{5}$ in. x $\frac{2}{25}$ in.). Pleat into a circle as for the first strip. Place the smaller circle on top of the larger circle. Trim the centre with a button made of paste. Cut two strips of paste 10 mm ($\frac{2}{5}$ in.) wide to resemble ribbons. One strip should be longer than the other. Attach them to the back of the rosette.

Use a clay gun to make four ropes by twisting paste of two different colours together. Drape the ropes from one rosette to the next.

Using flood icing, do the lettering as required. Place on the cake when dry.

Coming of age

Plates 20-21

Prepare and cover an oval petal cake measuring 340 mm (13 $\frac{3}{5}$ in.) in diameter.

Make the five pillars out of pastillage No. 2 using a mould. Leave to dry.

Model the figure's legs using pastillage No. 2. Model the feet using paste.

Mould the torso of the sitting figure (see *fig. 2f*, p. 10).

Trace the patterns for the guitar (see *pattern 7*, p. 72) onto thin cardboard and cut out. Cut the pattern pieces out of paste and assemble. A strip about 8 mm ($\frac{8}{25}$ in.) wide goes around the soundbox. Leave to dry. Paint to represent wood. Assemble and glue together with gum glue. Use fine cotton thread to make the strings.

To model the figure's arms and the hands, place the guitar across her lap. Position the arms and curve the fingers of the left hand around the neck of the instrument. Support the arms with polystyrene and leave to set.

When dry, remove the arms and guitar. Dress the figure as desired, allowing the feet to show (see Dressing a female figure, p. 16). Drape a scarf around the waist (see Special effects, p. 23).

Make the cushion by cutting two squares of the required size out of paste. Place a small piece of cotton wool in the centre of one square and place the other on top. Join all the edges. Place the figure on part of the cushion while it is still soft so that the cushion will mould around the body to look natural.

Make four scatter cushions as above. Decorate with thin strips of paste or with frills or other trimmings. Dust with pearl dust to resemble satin.

Make music sheets of paste, curling over some corners for a natural effect. When set, write the music score with a very fine non-toxic pen.

Place the columns into position and attach

with royal icing. Decorate with fine paste ribbons painted with russet iridescent colouring. Top each column with cascading flowers and leaves.

Make the birthday card using turquoise paste. Dab with different colours to create an antique look.

The wedding

Plates 22-25

Prepare and cover an oval cake measuring 460 mm x 330 mm ($18 \frac{2}{5}$ x $13 \frac{1}{5}$ in.).

Make the church scene at the base of the cake using pastillage No. 2 (see *pattern 8*, p. 73). Make the stained-glass windows (see *plate 24*, p. 51) out of sheet gelatine. Paint the inside of the windows with piping gel and colouring. Apply a strip of paste around each window. Attach to the inside of the wall with gum glue. Attach the wall to the side of the cake with royal icing. Add the roof, creating a thatched effect with royal icing.

Using paste, make the car using any small mould. Pipe tiny figures inside the car using royal icing. Airbrush the background on the side of the cake. Paint on the trees using royal icing. Add some leaves to the trees next to the church for a three-dimensional effect.

Mould the figures of the bride and groom (see Modelling the figure of a woman, p. 9, and Modelling the figure of a man, p. 10). Dress the bride and groom as required (see *plate 23*, p. 51). Complete dressing the groom before placing the bride's arms in position so that her hands can fit into his. Attach the figures to the cake with royal icing before assembling the gazebo.

To make the gazebo, cut a round polystyrene base measuring 200 mm (8 in.) in diameter x 30 mm ($1 \frac{1}{5}$ in.) high. Use thin cardboard templates as a guide for cutting the paste (see *pattern 9*, p. 73 and pastillage No. 2, p. 6).

Cut a 250 mm (10 in.) circle out of thin cardboard, slit to the centre and lap the ends to form a shallow cone. Secure with adhesive tape. Cut out a small pastillage disc, about 30 mm ($1 \frac{1}{5}$ in.) in diameter, and place in the tip of the cone.

Cut eight roof struts out of 2 mm ($\frac{2}{25}$ in.) thick pastillage (see *pattern 9a*, p. 73) and arrange at equal distances in the cone, attaching their pointed ends to the centre piece with gum glue. Allow to set.

Cut seven uprights out of 5 mm ($\frac{1}{5}$ in.) thick pastillage (see *pattern 9b*, p. 73), and the fence posts and bars out of 2 mm ($\frac{2}{25}$ in.) thick pastillage (see *patterns 9c-9d*, p. 73). Allow to set.

Arrange the uprights around the polystyrene base to coincide with the roof struts, attaching them with royal icing (the "missing" eighth upright forms the entrance to the gazebo). Lift the roof struts out of the cardboard mould and attach them to the uprights with royal icing.

Assemble the prepared parts of the fence. Make a handrail of paste in 35 mm ($1 \frac{2}{5}$ in.) lengths using a clay gun with a half-round disc (attach the pieces before completely set).

Decorate the struts with satinised paste ribbons and small modelled rose buds. Finish the top of the roof with small roses.

Make a flower girl and a pageboy (see Modelling the figure of a child, p. 11). The organza look of the flower girl's dress is achieved by giving her a pink underskirt and bodice topped with a white dress made of very thin paste.

To add interest, pipe a butterfly onto a flower in front of the children, and place a small bouquet next to the bride on the bench.

The nature lovers

Plate 26

The figures on this special cake had to be dressed in every detail as the people had been on the occasion they were celebrating. They loved nature and the outdoors, therefore this scene was created to encompass all of that.

Prepare and cover a round cake with a diameter of 250 mm (10 in.).

Make the log using pastillage No. 2. Decide where the man's foot will rest on the log and make a hole for the wire protruding from the foot.

Mould the figures of a man and a woman (see Modelling the figure of a man and Modelling the figure of a woman, pp. 9-10). Insert heavy wire into the legs, then bend the legs into position. Model the arms and allow them to dry in the correct positions on the figures. When set, remove and dress (see Basic dressing of a male figure and Basic dressing of a female figure, pp. 16-17).

To make the bracelets around the arms of the figures, use the smallest disc on the clay gun. Make a circle around the arm and glue the ends together. The bracelets must be loose on the arm. When dry, place a roll of wax paper around the arm under the bracelets and paint them gold and silver. Slide the paper away carefully to release the bracelets.

Make the watches of paste and place on the arms immediately.

To make the striped fabric for the woman's T-shirt, roll a piece of paste until paper thin. Use the smallest clay-gun disc to make stripes of coloured paste and place them on the rolled paste. Roll the fabric again to secure the stripes. Cut out the pieces of the garment. Keep them covered until needed so that they will remain pliable.

Make the soil of brown sugar, crumbled dry brown royal icing and dried herbs. Build a broken ant hill at the base of the tree trunk.

Pierrette and Pierrot

Plate 27

Prepare and cover a round cake with a diameter of 260 mm (10 $\frac{2}{5}$ in.). Cut out squares of black and white plastic icing for the floor. Mark a straight line across the centre of the cake. Following this line, place the squares into position. Cover the side of the cake and the board with black plastic icing.

Mould a Pierrette and Pierrot (see Modelling the figure of a woman and Modelling the figure of a man, pp. 9-10). For the seated figure make the legs separately, dressing the straight leg first. Dress and attach the crossed leg.

Using pastillage, make an open card by shaping the two sections separately and allowing them to dry. Pipe on the lettering as required. Join the two sections of the card at the spine using royal icing. Allow to set. Apply royal icing to the bottom edges and position the open card on the cake.

Using the semicircular disc in the clay gun, decorate the side of the cake with drapes consisting of two white pieces and one black piece. Attach with gum glue. Catch each drape with a miniature red rose.

Christmas cake

Plates 28-29

Prepare and cover a sculpted rectangular cake measuring 400 mm x 260 mm (16 in. x 10 $\frac{2}{5}$ in.). Mark the cake covering to resemble stonework. Decorate the cake board with holly and mistletoe. Using pastillage No. 2, make two shutters measuring 185 mm x 75 mm (7 $\frac{2}{5}$ in. x 3 in.) and place in position.

Make the face of Santa Claus using a suitable mould. Place a ball of paste in half of the right cheek (you are working in reverse) and the full

left cheek to obtain a face looking sideways. Leave to dry before painting the face.

Cover the pattern of Santa Claus (see *pattern 10*, p. 74) with strong, clear plastic. Place the moulded face in position. Model the left ear and place in position. Model the right and the left hand to just above the wrist, interlocking the hands in position on the pattern. Using red paste, model the right arm over the pattern. Flatten it to fit under the body. Model the right leg and place in position. Model the body and left leg, and place over the right arm and right leg. Model the left arm, flatten it slightly at the shoulder and place in position, covering the left wrist and moving the hands to interlock. When set, pipe the beard and the hair (see p. 17). Model the spectacles with fine fuse wire and place in position.

Cover the pattern of the deer (see *pattern 10*, p. 74) with strong, clear plastic. Using white paste, model the deer over the pattern. Paint as shown on *plate 29*, p. 54.

Cover the pattern of the stove (see *pattern 10*, p. 74) with strong, clear plastic. Model the stove over the pattern. Make other accessories as shown on *plate 29*, p. 54.

Japanese geisha girl

Plate 30

Prepare and cover an oval plaque measuring 270 mm x 206 mm (10 $\frac{4}{5}$ in. x 8 $\frac{6}{25}$ in.).

Mould the figure of a woman (see p. 9). Make the feet out of white paste and attach them to the base of the figure by pushing a toothpick through each heel. Make a division between the big toe and the other toes to represent the tabi socks worn by Japanese ladies.

Make soles resembling wood under the feet. Shape two rolls around a toothpick and place under the heel and the ball of the foot. Roll very thin thongs, place between the divided toes and attach the ends to either side of the shoe just short of the end of the heel.

Dress the figure in a kimono. This traditional garment worn by Japanese men and women comes in only one size. The length and width are adjusted at the waist, hence the fold of material below the obi (the black sash that is tied around the waist). As it is very difficult to dress the figure in a full-length kimono, we have made it in two parts.

Trace *pattern 11*, p. 75 onto thin cardboard and cut out. Cut the pattern pieces out of very thin paste.

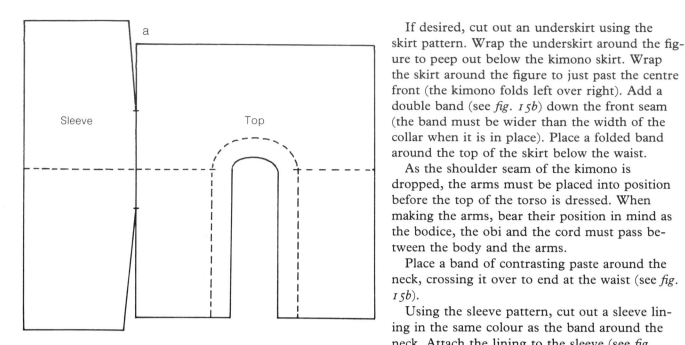

Sleeve

Top

Fig. 15
Dressing the geisha
girl.

b

Sleeve

Sleeve lining

Double band

c

If desired, cut out an underskirt using the skirt pattern. Wrap the underskirt around the figure to peep out below the kimono skirt. Wrap the skirt around the figure to just past the centre front (the kimono folds left over right). Add a double band (see *fig. 15b*) down the front seam (the band must be wider than the width of the collar when it is in place). Place a folded band around the top of the skirt below the waist.

As the shoulder seam of the kimono is dropped, the arms must be placed into position before the top of the torso is dressed. When making the arms, bear their position in mind as the bodice, the obi and the cord must pass between the body and the arms.

Place a band of contrasting paste around the neck, crossing it over to end at the waist (see *fig. 15b*).

Using the sleeve pattern, cut out a sleeve lining in the same colour as the band around the neck. Attach the lining to the sleeve (see *fig. 15b*). As the sleeve consists of one pattern piece, combining front and back, it must be draped very carefully over the arm to avoid breaking the fingers. Glue the side seams of the top together. Glue the sleeve seam under the arm (see *fig. 15c*).

Place a thin roll of paste in a contrasting colour around the torso just above the waist. Wrap the obi around the torso (see *fig. 15d*). (As the obi is stiff and does not show the waistline, it must be straight on the figure).

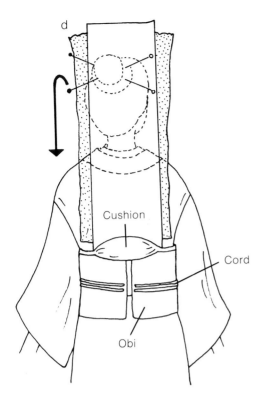

Using a clay gun, make a cord to go around the middle of the obi. Cut another strip of paste the same width as the obi and attach it vertically to the top edge of the obi (see *fig. 15d*), securing it with gum glue just below the shoulder blades. (If you are working with a dark on a light colour, place a piece of wax paper between the two to avoid discoloration.)

Make a cushion of paste with a slight kidney shape to attach above the waistline over the obi (see *fig. 15d*). Bring the flap down over the cushion and catch it with a fold below the obi, allowing the short flap to hang below it over the skirt (see *fig. 15e*).

Paint the kimono as desired. Place a fan in the geisha's hand (see p. 22). Geishas never wear jewellery but have swept-up hair and elaborate hair ornaments.

To make the bamboo screen, use the thick disc on the clay gun to make the frame. Roll the paste for the screens very thinly and attach them to the bamboo frame with strips of paste to represent ties. A simple bamboo table, cups, tea pot and kneeling cushions complete the scene.

Indian maiden

Plates 31-32

Prepare and cover an oval plaque measuring 270 mm x 205 mm (10 $\frac{4}{5}$ in. x 8 $\frac{1}{5}$ in.).

Mould the Indian maiden as for the Basic figure of a woman (see p. 9) with paste coloured as described on p. 9. Paint a red dot on her forehead and place a "jewel" in the side of her nose. Place flat sandals on her feet before dressing her. Dress her in an underskirt that is pleated below the waist and a top that ends just below the midriff (see *fig. 16a*). Dress the arms and place in position. Trim the top and the skirt as preferred. Do the hair in royal icing (see p. 17) before draping the sari.

To make the sari, cut out a piece of very thin paste measuring 300 mm x 110 mm (12 in. x 4 $\frac{2}{5}$ in.). Decorate with gold trimming as required. Beginning at the centre front of the waistline (see *fig. 16a*), drape the sari around the figure, pleating the fabric around to the right side. Wrap it around the body, draping it over to the left shoulder (see *fig. 16b*). Gather the drape and glue it to the shoulder with gum glue. Loosely drape the remaining length of the sari over the head, allowing it to fall in natural folds over the right arm (see *plate 32*, p. 56).

33

Fig. 16
Dressing the Indian
maiden.

Decorate the rest of the scene as preferred.
The maiden in *plate 31*, p. 56 is carrying a tray
of marigolds as part of a religious ceremony.

Clydesdale horses

Plate 33

This exhibit of Clydesdale horses was made by
Gay Prevost for the 1993 Cape Agricultural
Show, where it was awarded the trophy for Best
on Show in the Mexican technique section. The
scene depicts a ploughing competition at an agricultural show, hence the smartly clad farmer
wearing a tie and the horse brasses and trimmings on the pair of Clydesdales.

Prepare and cover a rectangular base measuring 850 mm x 400 mm (34 in. x 16 in.). Make the
very realistic soil by mixing cocoa into marzipan
for an interesting texture. Paint the centre of the
furrow with cocoa mixed with hot water to give
the darker look of turned soil. For added interest
to the soil, add herbs and pebbles of paste.

To model the horses, see Modelling horses,
p. 25. Secure the horses to the base with royal icing.

Make the small chains by stretching a piece of
cotton thread across a board. Secure with two
pins. Pipe dots onto the cotton. Paint when dry.
Leave to dry again, then turn and pipe the other
side.

Larger chains can be made by cutting out pastillage discs with holes in the centre. Shape each
circle into an oval. String the ovals together in a
straight line with dots of royal icing. Make loops
between the two ovals. Paint before turning to
make the loops on the other side. Ensure that it
is completely dry after painting and before handling it.

Model the farmer as described in Modelling
the figure of a man (see p. 10), leaving about
10 mm ($\frac{2}{5}$ in.) of wire protruding from the heel.

Dress him as described in Basic dressing of a male figure (see p. 17). Secure the figure by attaching the wire to the base.

The soiree

Plate 34

Prepare and cover an oval cake measuring 635 mm x 385 mm (25 $\frac{2}{5}$ in. x 15 $\frac{2}{5}$ in.). Use a mould to decorate the sides of the exhibit.

To make the piano, trace the pattern pieces (see *pattern 12*, p. 76) onto cardboard and cut out. Cut a 40 mm-thick (1 $\frac{3}{5}$ in.) dummy out of polystyrene (see pattern 12a [A-B-D-A]). Cut the pattern pieces out of 3 mm-thick ($\frac{3}{25}$ in.) pastillage.

Note Use the full *pattern 12a* (A-B-D-A) for the bottom of the piano and E-C-D-E for the top. *Patterns 12b-12c* should be cut in one piece and wrapped around the polystyrene dummy from A-D (hold in position with pieces of sponge and allow to dry). The pattern piece for the keyboard should be about 3 mm ($\frac{3}{25}$ in.) narrower than A-B-C-E on *pattern 12a*, and the front pattern piece below the keyboard about 3 mm ($\frac{3}{25}$ in.) narrower than the lid.

Use a clay gun and large trefoil disc to make the legs (see measurements in bottom left-hand corner of p. 76).

Trim the sides of the piano with pipe work.

Make a round, padded piano stool. Make the legs using a clay gun. Ensure that the stool is the correct height for the figure sitting at the piano. Place the pianist (see below) on the stool while still wet to ensure that she will sit properly when dry.

Make two chairs out of pastillage (see *pattern 13*, p. 77).

Make and dress the three musicians (see Basic dressing of a female figure and Basic dressing of a male figure, pp. 16-17). Make a violin and allow the violinist's hand to set around the neck of the instrument. Let the flautist's hand dry while holding the flute.

Invitation to the dance

Plates 35-36

Prepare and cover an oval plaque measuring 380 mm x 270 mm (15 $\frac{1}{5}$ in. x 10 $\frac{4}{5}$ in.).

To make the crinoline lady, mould a female figure of paste (see Modelling the figure of a woman, p. 9). Make an underskirt of pastillage by moulding it over an empty 1 litre cool-drink bottle. When set, bend the arm wires up and lower the skirt over the body. Fill in the gap from the waist to the top of the skirt with gum paste (see *fig. 17*). Smooth the gum paste neatly up against the body towards the waist (always apply gum glue to the figure, not to the piece that is being attached).

Glue a lace frill around the base of the under-skirt. Cut a skirt out of paste and gather it at the waist. Roll the paste at the waist to reduce the thickness. Recut the waist and glue it into position on the figure. To keep the waist small, attach the skirt just below the waistline. Catch the skirt hem into position with gum glue. Finish the side of the skirt with frills (see *plate 35*, p. 58).

Glue the back of the bodice in position. Glue the front of the bodice in position, making sure the bodice just meets the skirt without overlapping it.

Attach the arms to the torso. Make and attach lace frills to cover the top of the arms.

Make ribbon trims using maroon paste brushed with russet pearl dust.

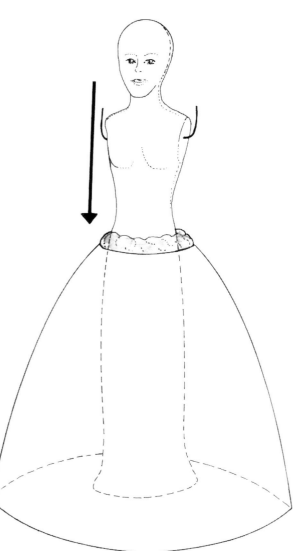

Fig. 17
The underskirt of the crinoline dress is lowered over the figure and attached below the waist.

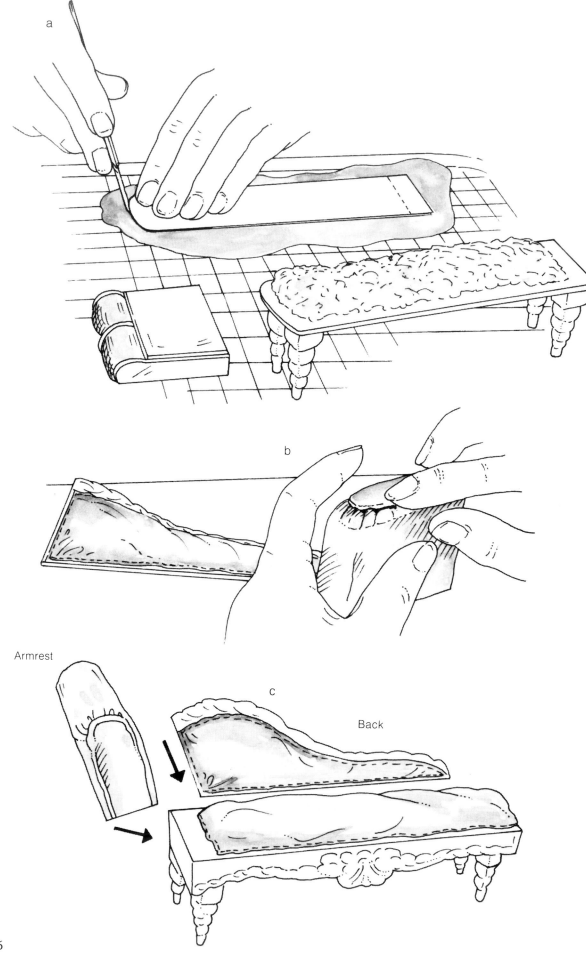

Fig. 18
Upholstering and assembling the chaise longue.

a

b

Armrest

c

Back

36

Embroider the dress with royal icing and paint with silver.

To make the soldier, mould a male figure of paste (see Modelling the figure of a man, p. 10). Make the legs (see p. 11). Attach tights to just below the knee. Make Hessian boots that fit over the tights using very thin black paste.

Dress the soldier (see Dressing a male figure, p. 17). Cut out the lower back of the jacket to hang below the hollow of the knee and to be wide enough to fold around the body to about 8 mm ($\frac{8}{25}$ in.) on either side of the centre front. Line with white paste, fold the corners to the centre back and catch with a tiny disc of paste to resemble a button (see *plate 36*, p. 58).

Cut out the upper back of the jacket and glue into position. Cut out the jacket front to end at the waist and glue into position. Decorate with braid made of gum paste. Attach the collar and decorate.

Place the sash, which forms part of the belt, across the chest and back and attach the sword.

Dress the arms and set into position. Make epaulettes and attach to the shoulders. Paint all decorations gold.

Make a shawl, handbag, shako (a tall, cylindrical, high-crowned hat with a peaked brim) and a pair of gloves. Place on the chaise longue.

To make the chaise longue, use either *pattern 14* or a suitable mould, which will give the mouldings as in *plate 35*, p. 58. If the mould is used, Nos. 2, 3, 4 and 7 of *pattern 14* will not be required.

If the mould is not used, trace and cut out all the pattern pieces and pipe the mouldings on with royal icing. Place the templates under a sheet of glass and secure with adhesive tape. Roll out pastillage No. 2 to 2 mm ($\frac{2}{25}$ in.) thick and cut out all the pieces for the chaise longue. Dust the glass with cornflour and place the cut-out pieces on the patterns to ensure that they fit. Leave to dry, turning regularly to prevent warping.

Assemble the chaise longue (see *fig. 18a-c*). Paint gum glue within the dotted line on the seat (template No. 1). Cut a piece of cotton wool to size and place on the gum glue (see *fig. 18a*). Roll out a piece of paste and, using template No. 1 up to the broken line, cut out the seat's upholstery. This "fabric" can be textured by using a ridged roller or can be mottled with pastes of various colours (see Special effects, p. 23). Attach the fabric to the seat over the cotton wool by glueing around the padding on the dotted lines (see *fig. 18c*).

Assemble the armrest, using templates Nos. 4, 5 and 6. Attach two pieces of template 4 to either end of template No. 5 with the rounded sections facing towards the front and the bottom ends meeting. Pipe the third piece of template No. 4 onto the centre. Make small rolls of paste and place between these supports when dry. Place template No. 6 onto the supports just below the rounded tops (see *fig. 18a*). Leave to dry thoroughly.

If the mould is used, make eight half-legs. When dry, join two halves together with royal icing. Leave to dry again. Smooth the edges using an emery board or sandpaper. Mould two pattern pieces each of Nos. 2 and 3, and join together to form a rectangle. Allow to set while upside down. Place the legs in position at each corner, joining with royal icing. Leave to dry. When set, turn the chaise longue over and stand it on its legs. Place the padded seat (see *fig. 18c*) on top and attach with royal icing. Upholster the back up to the moulding (see *fig. 18c*).

If the pattern pieces only are used, make a rectangle of templates Nos. 2 and 3. Leave to dry. Glue the padded seat (template No. 1) onto the legs. Leave to dry again. Pad the back (template No. 7) and cover with paste, taking the paste over the top to the back. Attach with gum glue.

Regardless of the method used, complete the chaise longue by attaching cotton wool to the front of the armrest with gum glue (see *fig. 18b*). Cut out paste and attach with gum glue, covering the cotton wool and bringing the paste over the top to below the rounded section. Attach another piece of paste over the lower back section down to the base. Attach the edges with gum glue, folding them over to the middle of the side piece. Attach a small piece of cotton wool to fit over this. Cut another piece of upholstery using template No. 5 and glue it over the padding to neaten (see *fig. 18b*).

Place the armrest and back in position and attach with royal icing (see *fig. 18c*). Prop up until completely dry. Neaten the back of the chaise longue by covering it with a piece of paste upholstery. Trim as desired using a clay gun.

Fig. 19a
Add a shoe, Garrett frill
and bustle to the basic
female figure.

The conversation

Plates 37-38

Prepare and cover an oval plaque measuring
270 x 200 mm (10 $\frac{4}{5}$ in. x 8 in.).

To make the lady with the parasol, mould the
figure of a woman (see p. 9). Make the bustle before beginning to dress the figure. Take a
walnut-sized piece of paste and roll it into a ball.
Flatten one side of the ball and glue it to the
back of the figure (see *fig. 19a*). Always apply
gum glue to the figure, never to the piece that
will be attached.

Glue one foot to the base of the figure (see *fig.
19a*). Attach the frills as instructed in Basic
dressing of a female figure (see *fig. 19b*). Attach
the skirt front and back. If it is to be pleated, use
a toothpick to form each pleat. Roll the waistline
of the skirt to flatten it before placing it on the
figure.

Fold the drape (see *fig. 19c*). Place the centre
front of the drape on the centre front of the skirt
and take it around to the back (see *fig. 19d*). Remember to apply glue wherever the drape must
stick.

Attach all the trimmings to the train. If the
train will have a frilled hem, glue the frill into
position before attaching the train to the skirt
over the bustle (see *fig. 19e-f*).

Place the frilled neckpiece in position (see *fig.
19g*).

Cut out the bodice back to be longer than the
waistline. Make a slit 10 mm ($\frac{2}{5}$ in.) from the bottom at the centre back to part over the bustle
(see *fig. 19h*).

Cut out the bodice front and place into
position.

Attach the trimmings below the bustle.

To make a three-quarter sleeve, attach a frill
in position over the gloved arm. If the figure
should wear gloves, mould the arms and hands
in the colour of the gloves.

To complete the scene, model the figure of the
man (see p. 10) and dress him as described in Basic dressing of a male figure (see p. 17). Model
the dog (see p. 24) and make a lamppost and
wrought-iron fence.

Fig. 19b
Attach frills as required
around the base of the
figure.

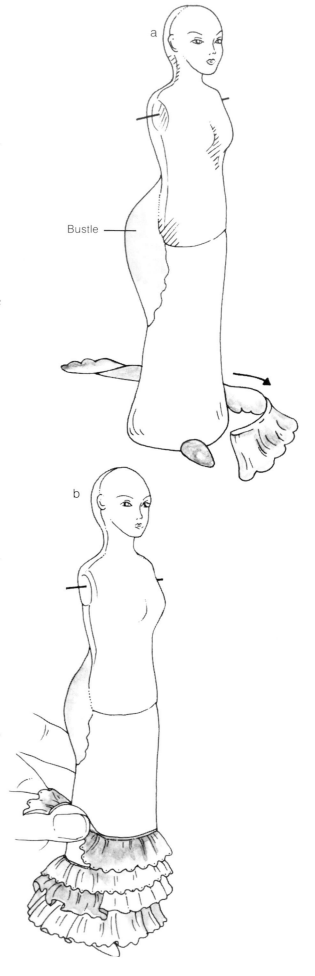

38

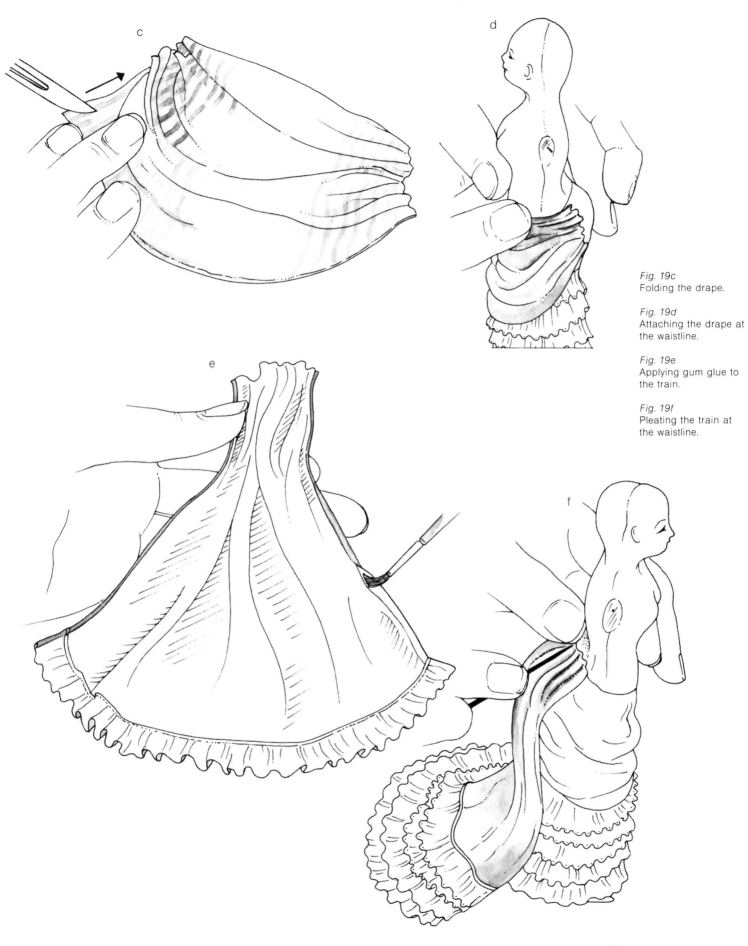

Fig. 19c
Folding the drape.

Fig. 19d
Attaching the drape at
the waistline.

Fig. 19e
Applying gum glue to
the train.

Fig. 19f
Pleating the train at
the waistline.

39

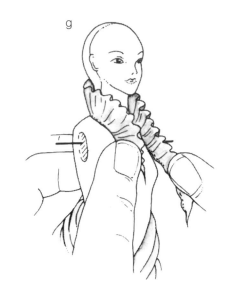

g

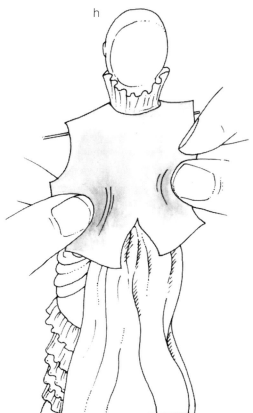

h

Fig. 19g
Attaching a frill at the neckline.

Fig. 19h
Making a slit in the bodice back to fit over the bustle.

The clowns

Plate 39

This charming example of Mexican sugar art won Cynthia Fletcher a second prize at the 1993 Cape Show.

The base is 300 mm (12 in.) in diameter. Wilton human moulds were used for the bodies and the Zimbabwe Willis clown mould was used for the masks.

The balls and drums were made of pastillage. To make the balls, mould two halves over a spherical shape and join together with royal icing when dry. Decorate as desired.

The milliner

Plates 40-41

This exhibit was made in collaboration with Cynthia Fletcher and Frances Bell.

Prepare and cover a quadrant cake or base measuring 605 mm x 395 mm x 230 mm (24 $\frac{1}{5}$ in. x 15 $\frac{4}{5}$ in. x 9 $\frac{1}{5}$ in.).

Using pastillage No. 1, cut out three walls. Texture one wall by rolling with a ridged roller and decorate the other two with drapes of coloured paste. Allow to dry completely before attaching to the base at right angles using royal icing.

Trace the pattern pieces for the mirror (*pattern 15*, p. 79), chest of drawers (*pattern 16*, pp. 80-81) and stool (*pattern 17*, p. 82) onto cardboard and cut out. Cut the pieces out of pastillage No. 2.

To assemble the mirror, place a 24-gauge wire vertically between two pieces of the mirror stand and set with royal icing. Repeat with the two remaining uprights. Leave to dry. Repeat with the pieces of the cross bar, allowing 5 mm ($\frac{1}{5}$ in.) of wire to protrude at either end.

Attach another piece of wire across the mirror where indicated by the dotted line, allowing 5 mm ($\frac{1}{5}$ in.) of wire to protrude at either end. Join the two mirror pieces with royal icing. When dry, insert the wire of the cross bar into the hole at the base of the stand. Insert the mirror wire into the centre hole of the stand. Secure both wires with royal icing. Place the second stand in position, inserting the wires into the appropriate holes. Secure with royal icing. Allow to dry standing upright with the mirror set at the correct angle. Support both stands and the mirror until dry. Apply pearl dust to the mirror to give a polished effect.

To assemble the chest of drawers, follow the

numerical sequence on *pattern 16* (attach the assembled drawer sides and base [Nos. 5 and 6] to the drawer front along the dotted lines on pattern piece No. 7). Leave one drawer open to fill with hats. Decorate as desired with knobs and piping.

To assemble the stool, place the cut-out pieces on a flat surface. Glue together the front, the side pieces and the back at right angles using royal icing. Leave to dry completely. Upholster the seat of the stool as for the chaise longue (see p. 37). Place the seated figure on the stool while the upholstery is still soft to make a natural-looking indentation.

To assemble the three-legged hat stand, glue the three sections of *pattern 18* together using royal icing. Support until dry. Attach hat pegs made with a clay gun to the stand.

Make as many hats as required for the hat stand and to place on the chest of drawers. Make an oval frilled rug of paste.

Mould the milliner and seated lady (see Modelling the figure of a woman, p. 9) and dress as preferred (see Basic dressing of a female figure, p. 16).

The doll maker

Plates 42-48

Prepare and cover a cake or base measuring 605 mm x 395 mm x 230 mm (24 $\frac{1}{5}$ in. x 15 $\frac{4}{5}$ in. x 9 $\frac{1}{5}$ in.).

To frame the scene, cut three walls out of 5 mm-thick ($\frac{1}{5}$ in.) pastillage. Allow to dry on glass, turning regularly to prevent warping. When dry, decorate the walls by stencilling (see *pattern 4*, p. 69). Spread pink icing over all the bows and ribbons. Cover the dots with yellow. Lift the stencil carefully. Embroider white and lavender royal icing forget-me-nots around each yellow centre.

Place a shelf, clothes-rack and plaque in position before assembling the walls. Allow to set completely before placing dolls' heads on the shelves and hanging dresses on the clothes-rack.

Make the armchair out of pastillage No. 2 (see *pattern 19*, pp. 83-85). Follow the letter sequence to assemble the frame and the numerical sequence for the upholstery. Glue the chair pieces together with royal icing and the upholstery with gum glue.

Make the upright chair (see *pattern 20*, p. 86) out of pastillage. Paint to resemble wood.

Make two tables out of pastillage. Throw a tablecloth made of paste over one table.

Make the pram (see *pattern 21*, p. 86) and the rocking horse (see *pattern 22*, p. 87) out of pastillage.

Make the chest of drawers (see *pattern 16*, p. 80-81) out of pastillage, following the instructions as given for *The Milliner* (see p. 40-41). Leave one drawer open. Colour paste in various colours and roll out to resemble lengths of dress fabric. Drape these in the open drawer of the chest.

Mould the doll maker, following the instructions for a seated figure (see p. 10). Apply make-up following the instructions for ageing (see p. 15). To ensure that the figure's arms will be in the correct position, seat the doll maker on the chair at the table before making the arms. Make her spectacles of fuse wire. Pipe her hair of grey royal icing. Place the spectacles in position while the hair is still wet.

Using a clay gun and royal icing, make the wigs in the box on the table. Make the dolls by casting heads in moulds of different sizes. Model the bodies and legs of the dolls as for children (see p. 11). Allow the pram and armchair to dry completely before dressing the dolls that will sit in them. When dressed, place all the dolls in position immediately so that the clothes will mould into the chair and pram and look natural.

Make the dolls' dresses over hangers and place in position when dry. Make the wigs and hats on stands as well as the dolls' arms and legs and other decorations (see *plate 48*, p. 63).

Show boat

Plate 49

Prepare a styrofoam base consisting of two parts. For the first part, cut a piece of styrofoam 90 mm × 450 mm × 20 mm and cover with blue plastic icing to represent water. (This forms the base on which *Cotton Blossom* will be assembled.) Cut a second piece of styrofoam 250 mm × 450 mm × 30 mm and cover with brown plastic icing. Mark to resemble the wooden slats of the quay.

Cut two blocks of styrofoam 9 mm × 6 mm × 4 mm and cover with beige plastic icing to resemble bales of cotton. Stencil the word COTTON on top.

Trace the pattern pieces for *Cotton Blossom* (see *pattern 23*, p. 89-98) onto thin cardboard and cut out. Trace and cut out separate templates for the doors and windows. Cut out stencils of each deck's assembly lines to use as a guide when assembling the pieces.

Cut a solid disc out of 10 mm-thick pastillage for the paddle wheel (No. 18). Cut all other pattern pieces out of 5 mm-thick pastillage, including inner wall supports (see *The Victorian house,* p. 43), pillars and balustrade uprights. Allow to dry, turning every day to avoid warping.

To make the gangplank, colour a small piece of pastillage brown, roll out and cut to measure 30 mm × 50 mm. Make two rough, round rope posts measuring 40 mm × 10 mm to stand on the quay.

Cut out three decks (No. 1A-1C) 420 mm long and one top deck (No. 1D) 390 mm long. Attach all windows and doors in position on the walls before assembling the boat.

Assembling the boat

To assemble the boat, follow the numerical sequence of the pattern pieces. Use royal icing to join the sections.

Place one of the three large decks (No. 1A) in position on the "water", flush with the back of the base, leaving a 15 mm gap between the water and the quay (this will allow space for the paddle wheel). Secure with royal icing.

Place the fascia (No. 2) around the base of the bottom deck, starting at the rear and following the curve to the front as far as the assembly line. When dry, place the floor of the bottom deck (No. 1B) on top of the fascia and leave to set.

Use the stencil of the bottom deck to mark out the assembly lines of the walls. Attach inner wall supports.

Place the bottom deck front wall (No. 3) on the marked assembly line, followed by walls No. 4 and No. 5.

Place the middle deck (No. 1C) in position on top of the bottom structure. Mark the assembly line using the stencil for the middle deck. Place walls Nos. 6, 7, 8 and 9 in position, adding inner wall supports.

Place the top deck (No. 1D) in position. Mark the assembly lines using the stencil for the top deck.

To form the bridge cabin, place walls Nos. 10, 11 and 12 in position, adding inner wall supports. Place roof No. 13 in position.

Place wall No. 14 in position at the front, and backing panel No. 15 at the back, followed by backing panel No. 16 at the right side.

Cover all wall joins with paste using a clay gun and a size 2 trefoil disc.

Cover the pillar fronts (No. 20A-B) using a clay gun and half a round disc, decorating the tops with the moulding of your choice.

Set the balustrade uprights (No. 17) into position. When set, add trimmings made with a clay gun and a No. 2 round disc. When dry, make the balustrade railings using half a round disc. Place on the supports before completely set, in

case adjustments have to be made. When the railings have set attach life belts (No. 22) as desired.

Decorate the front wall (No. 7) with moulding and a trimming scroll on which to hang a small, moulded bell.

Decorate the paddle wheel (No. 18) as preferred. Attach the plaque (No. 21) and window (No. 19) to the wheelhouse wall (No. 14).

Before making the seated girl, cut a piece of polystyrene the height of the cotton bale. Using pastillage, model the base for the girl on the polystyrene (see Modelling the figure of a woman, p. 9). Make a skirt for the girl (see Basic dressing of a female figure, p. 16). Paint gum glue down the back from the waist to the hollow of the knee. Attach the skirt to the figure. Place the figure back in position on the piece of polystyrene. This will allow the skirt to fall in natural folds, which can be arranged as you wish. Glue the side seams to the base. Fold over the front of the skirt. Dress the rest of the figure as for Basic dressing of a female figure (see p. 16).

For the seated man, make the lower legs and feet of paste (see Modelling the figure of a man, p. 10). Make the upper legs and body of pastillage and attach to the lower legs with wire. Place the arms in position on the figure with the hand around the knife and allow to set. Remove the arms when dry and dress. Model the standing man, remembering to insert heavy-gauge wire in the bent leg. Add other figures as desired.

The Victorian house

Plates 50-55

To construct this intricate example of structural Mexican sugar at least six times the quantity of the Pastillage No. 1 recipe (see p. 5) will be required. Mix double quantities of the recipe at a time, adding the desired colouring at the creamy mixture stage. Mix the batches together afterwards. Initially the colour should be darker than required, as it will become lighter when extra icing sugar is added. More pastillage may be required to complete the house.

Prepare and cover a rectangular base measuring 870 mm x 580 mm (34 $\frac{4}{5}$ in. x 23 $\frac{1}{5}$ in.).

Trace all the plans for the house (see *pattern 24,* p. 100-149). Paste onto cardboard and cut out. Assemble the cardboard pieces before starting on the sugar modelling to familiarise yourself with the construction of the house. A good idea would be to cut out two sets of patterns, leaving the completed cardboard house as a guide.

To prepare the house, cut all the walls, foundations, supports and roof pieces out of 5 mm-thick ($\frac{1}{5}$ in.) pastillage No. 1. Chamfer the edges where required. Place on glass and allow to dry for at least a week, turning the pieces each day to prevent warping.

Mould the pillars and cut out the veranda railings. When completely dry, decorate the walls with slats of gum paste. Trim the windows with gum paste (a clay gun is excellent for this). Cut out circles and decorate the front bay-window walls. Attach thin plastic or sheet gelatine to resemble windowpanes on the inside of the walls. Paint the arched windowpanes to represent stained glass. Drape paste curtains over the inside of the windows. Place the doors in position. Trim the gable with a moulded piece of paste. Mould and pipe the inner decorations. Apply the roof tiles with gum paste, making sure the lower edge is of the same colour as the tiles. Cover the foundation with paste to resemble brickwork.

To assemble the house, mark the outline of the floor plan on a board covered with plastic icing. Secure the floor pieces with royal icing. *Note* The floor ends 6 mm ($\frac{6}{25}$ in.) from the outline of

the house to accommodate the thickness of the walls. Pipe the large east wall in position. Pipe the wall supports into place (see A on fig. 20). Continue to the south elevation, piping the supports into position as you progress. When the bay walls are in place set the gable into position. Using paste, form the fish-scale pattern on the decorative section of the gable. Cut 5 mm-wide ($\frac{1}{5}$ in.) strips out of very thin paste and use to cover all the wall joins. Mould the corbel and set in position around the house under the eaves.

Pipe the verandas and stairs into position. When set, apply the cast pillars and upright supports for the veranda railings. It is best to make the parallel bars when you are ready to assemble them; allow to dry for 15 minutes before piping into position. This will allow for a certain amount of flexibility should you need to make any adjustments.

To assemble the roof, pipe the roof supports into position (see B and C on fig. 20). Set roof pieces E and F into position, making sure the apex of the roof matches. Set the west gable into position (Nos. 7 and 11), recessing it by 30 mm (1 $\frac{1}{5}$ in.). Set the top south gable into position

43

(Nos. 16 and 17), recessing it by 10 mm ($\frac{2}{5}$ in.). Pipe the lower south gable into position (Nos. 20 and 17), recessing it by 10 mm ($\frac{2}{5}$ in.). Pipe J and H over the west gable. Pipe D against F and E. Set B and C into position followed by A. Pipe M and G into position. Pipe the pieces of the veranda roof into position. Place L and K in position over the front porch. Pipe the lightning arresters into position. Set the chimneys in place. Trim the doors with handles and add a knocker to the front door.

Decorate the scene as desired with figures and a landscaped garden.

Plates

Plate 10
A special christening cake. Make up the doll's face to resemble the baby.

Plate 11
A doll's wardrobe, a birthday cake for a pre-teen girl.

Plate 12
The magician, a birthday cake for a 10-year-old boy.

Plate 13
Miss Muffet.

Plate 14
Three little girls on a
birthday cake.

Plate 15
Close-up of the
banner.

Plate 16
Close-up of donkey's-
tail party game.

Plate 17
Close-up of little girl
carrying a birthday
cake.

Plate 18
Close-up of little girl
opening gifts.

48

Plate 19
The rugby player, a birthday cake for a sports-mad boy.

Plate 20
The scene of a girl playing a guitar – for a twenty-first birthday cake.

Plate 21
Back view of the guitar player.

Plate 22
The wedding cake.

Plate 23
Back view of the bride.

Plate 24
Close-up of the church.

Plate 25
Close-up of the flower girl and pageboy.

Plate 26
Two nature lovers meet in the veld.

Plate 27
Pierrette and Pierrot.

Plate 28
The Christmas cake.

Plate 29
Close-up of decorations for the Christmas cake.

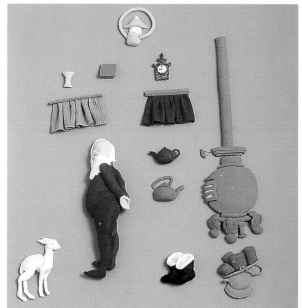

Plate 30
A Japanese geisha girl prepares a tea ceremony.

Plate 31
An Indian maiden bringing an offering.

Plate 32
Close-up of the back of the Indian maiden.

Plate 33
Two Clydesdale horses
ploughing a field.

Plate 34
A musical evening.

Plate 35
Invitation to the dance.

Plate 36
Close-up of back view of the soldier's coat.

Plate 37
A lady in a bustle dress with a parasol, in conversation with a gentleman.

Plate 38
Close-up of the back of the bustle dress.

Plate 39
The clowns, a scene for a birthday cake for a young boy.

Plate 40
In the milliner's hat shop.

Plate 41
Close-up of the milliner and a customer trying on hats.

Plate 42
The doll maker in her workroom.

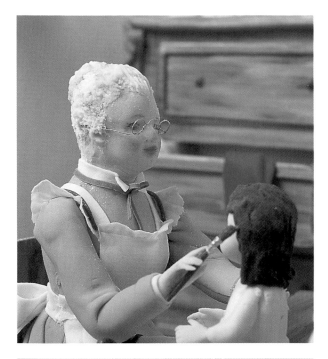

Plate 43
Close-up of the doll maker at work.

Plate 44
Two dolls on an armchair.

Plate 45
Dolls' dresses hanging from the clothes-rack.

Plate 46
Close-up of the working table.

Plate 47
A doll in a pram.

Plate 48
Close-up of half-completed dolls.

Plate 49
The show boat *Cotton Blossom*.

Plate 50
The Victorian house.

Plate 51
The west and south elevations.

Plate 52
The west elevation.

Plate 53
Detail of the south elevation.

Plate 54
The south and east elevations.

Plate 55
The north and west elevations.

Patterns

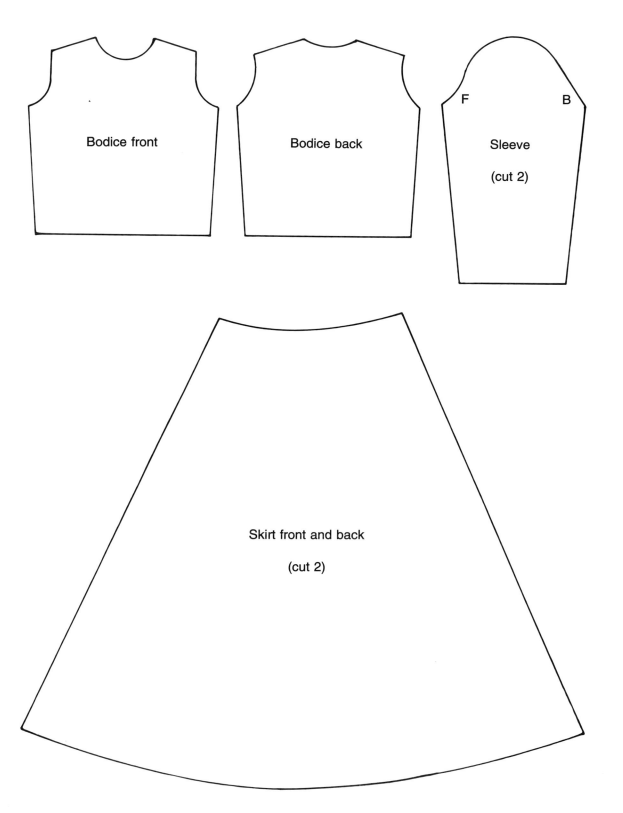

Bodice front

Bodice back

Sleeve

(cut 2)

F   B

Pattern 1
Basic pattern pieces for a woman's dress.

Skirt front and back

(cut 2)

Pattern 2
Basic pattern pieces for
men's clothing.

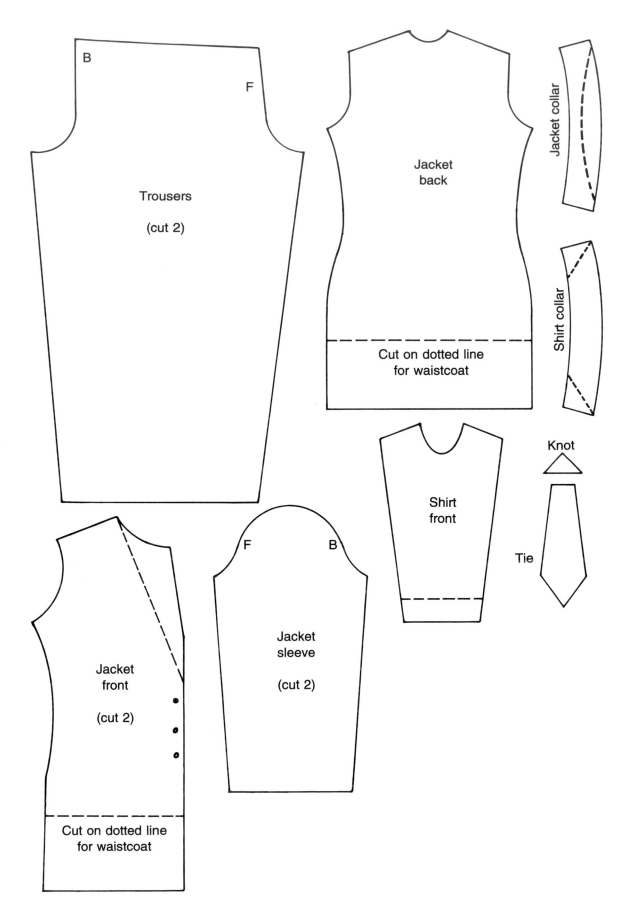

B

F

Trousers

(cut 2)

Jacket
back

Jacket collar

Shirt collar

Cut on dotted line
for waistcoat

Knot

Shirt
front

Tie

Jacket
front

(cut 2)

F   B

Jacket
sleeve

(cut 2)

Cut on dotted line
for waistcoat

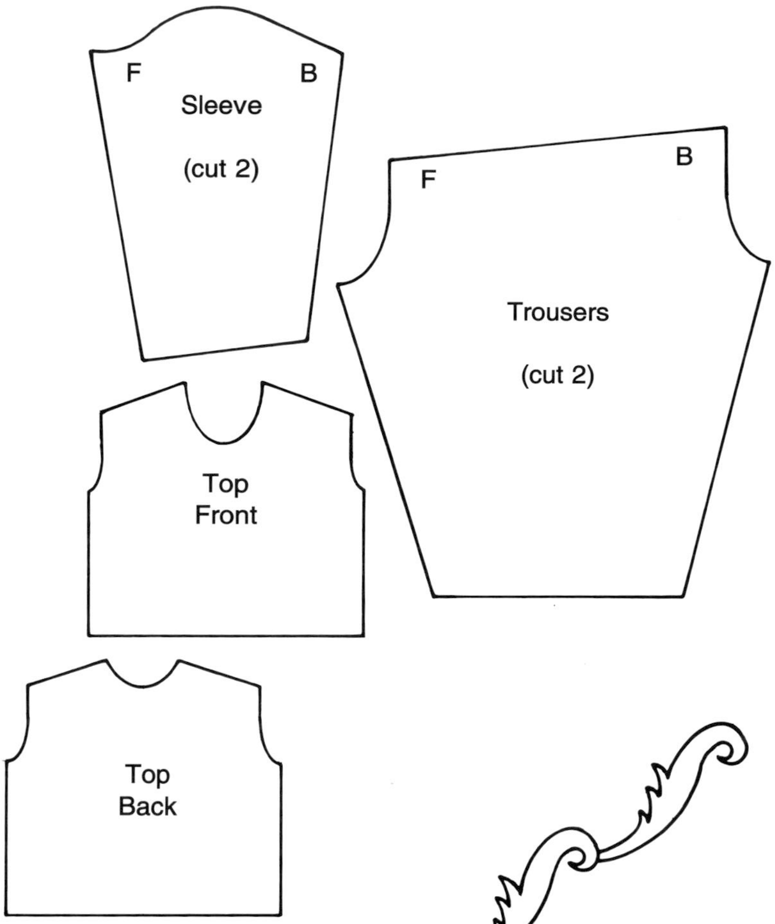
F
B
Sleeve
(cut 2)
F
B
Trousers
(cut 2)
Top
Front
Top
Back

Pattern 3
Basic pattern pieces for children's clothing.

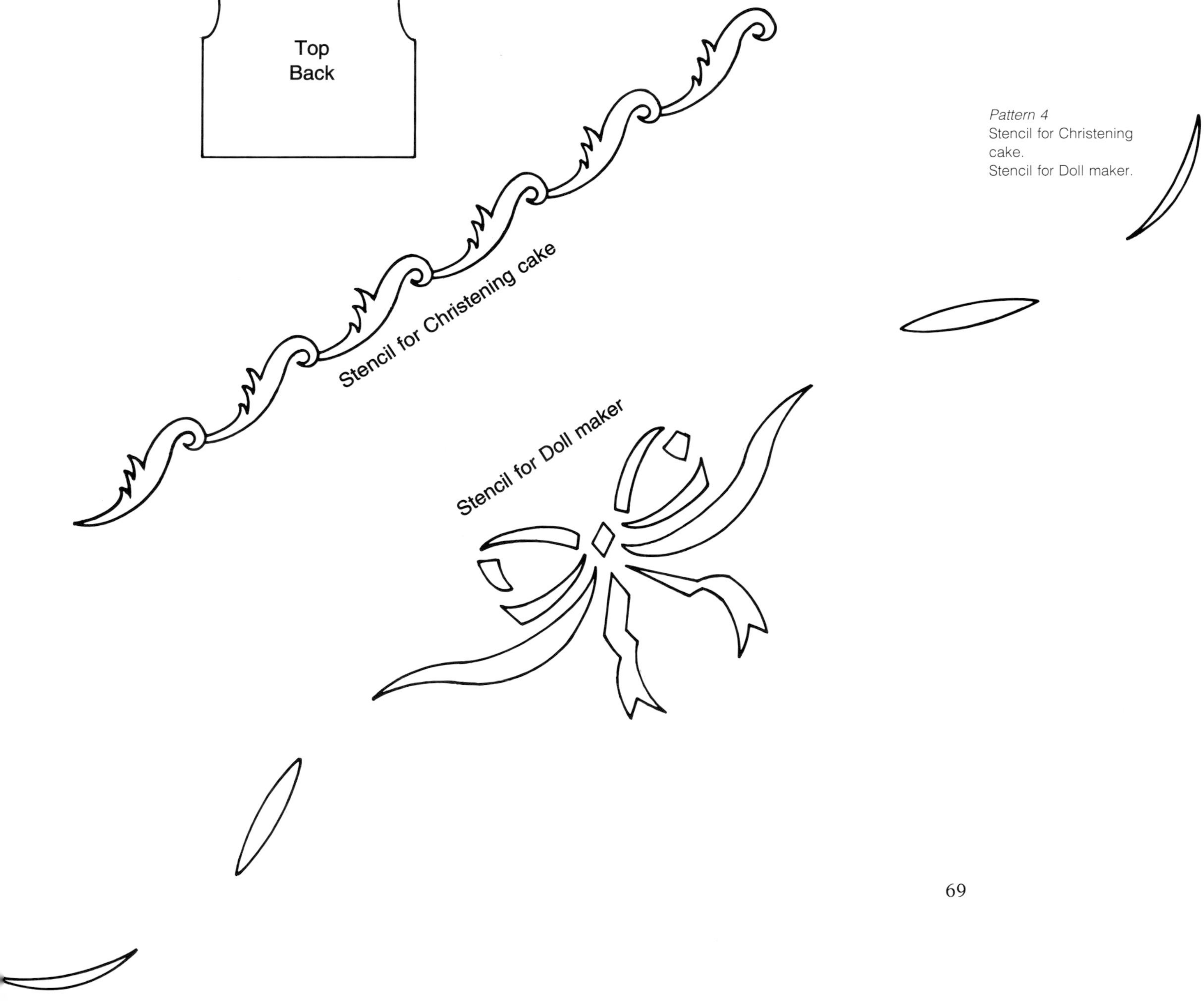
Stencil for Christening cake
Stencil for Doll maker

Pattern 4
Stencil for Christening cake.
Stencil for Doll maker.

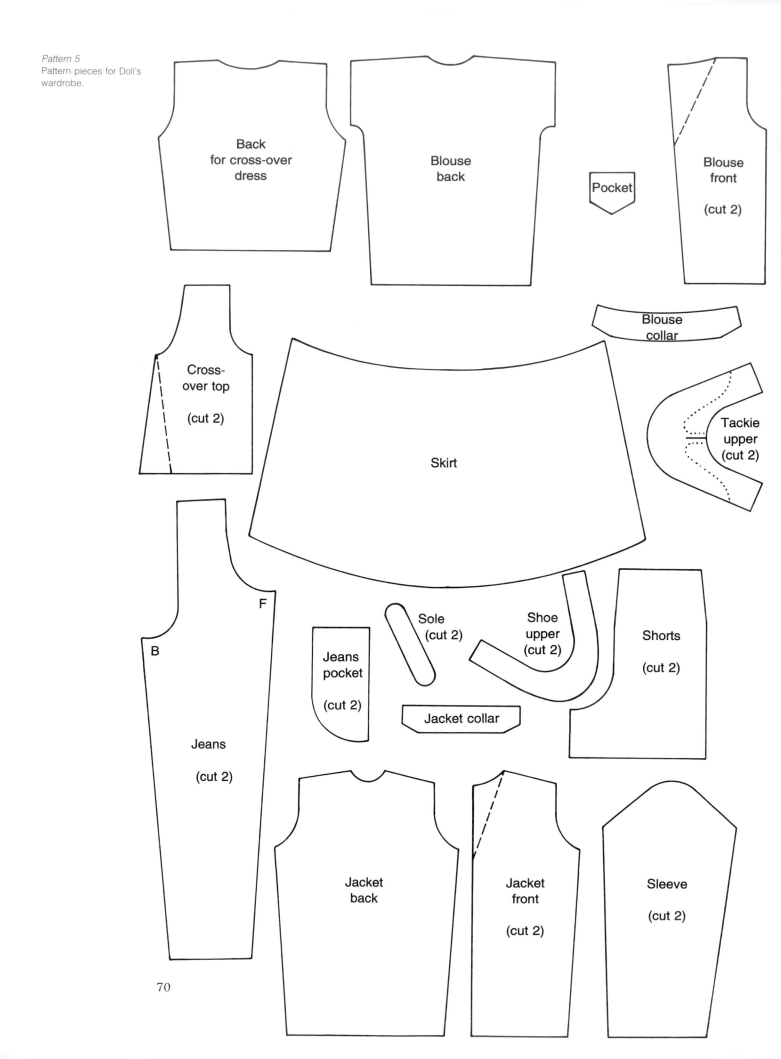

Back
for cross-over
dress

Blouse
back

Pocket

Blouse
front

(cut 2)

Cross-
over top

(cut 2)

Blouse
collar

Skirt

Tackie
upper
(cut 2)

F

B

Sole
(cut 2)

Shoe
upper
(cut 2)

Shorts

(cut 2)

Jeans
pocket

(cut 2)

Jacket collar

Jeans

(cut 2)

Jacket
back

Jacket
front

(cut 2)

Sleeve

(cut 2)

Pattern 6
Side pictures for birthday
cake with three little girls.

71

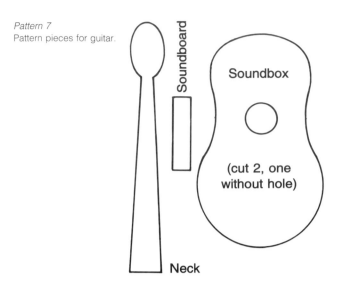

Soundboard

Soundbox

(cut 2, one
without hole)

Neck

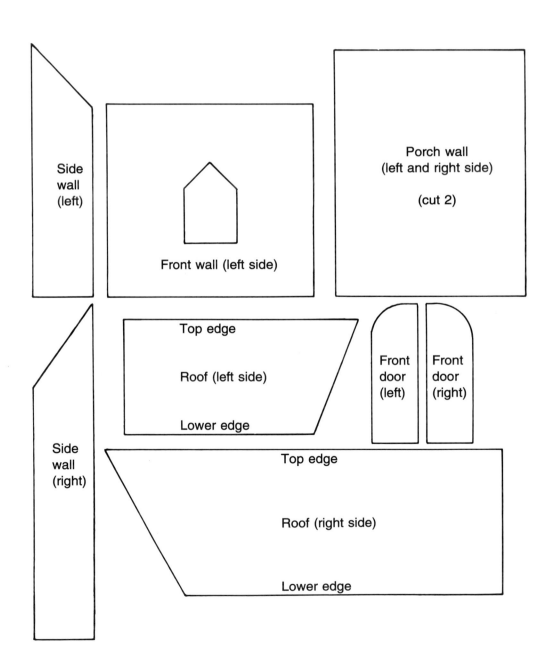

Side
wall
(left)

Porch wall
(left and right side)

(cut 2)

Front wall (left side)

Side
wall
(right)

Top edge

Roof (left side)

Lower edge

Front
door
(left)

Front
door
(right)

Top edge

Roof (right side)

Lower edge

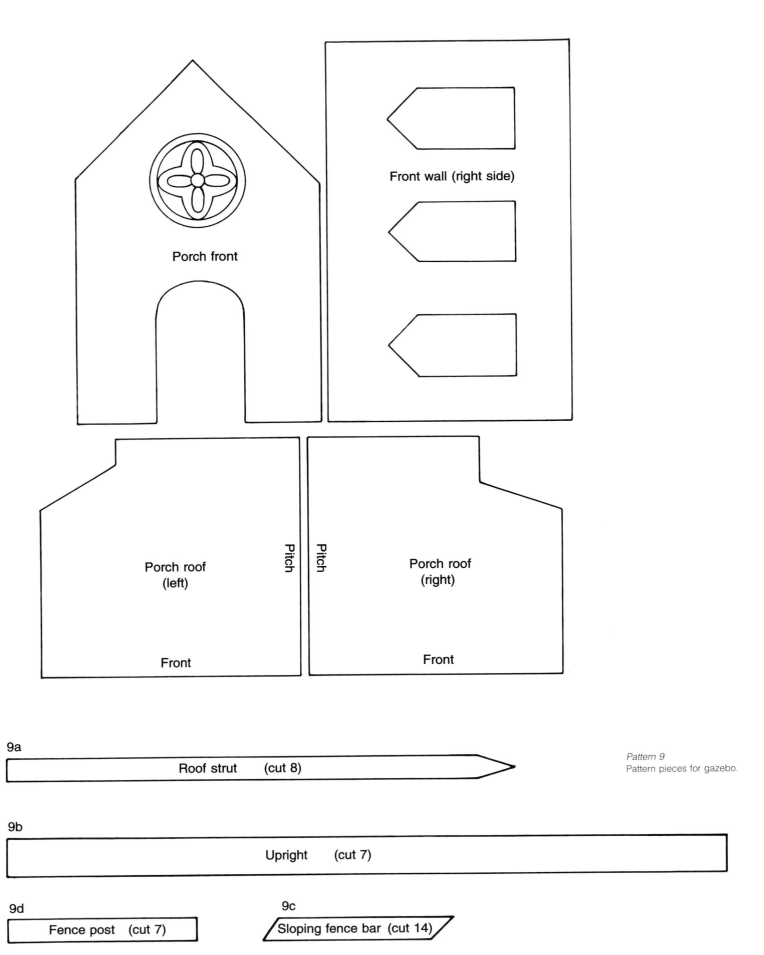

Porch front

Front wall (right side)

Porch roof
(left)

Pitch

Pitch

Porch roof
(right)

Front

Front

9a

Roof strut   (cut 8)

Pattern 9
Pattern pieces for gazebo.

9b

Upright   (cut 7)

9d

Fence post   (cut 7)

9c

Sloping fence bar (cut 14)

73

Deer

Stove

Santa Claus

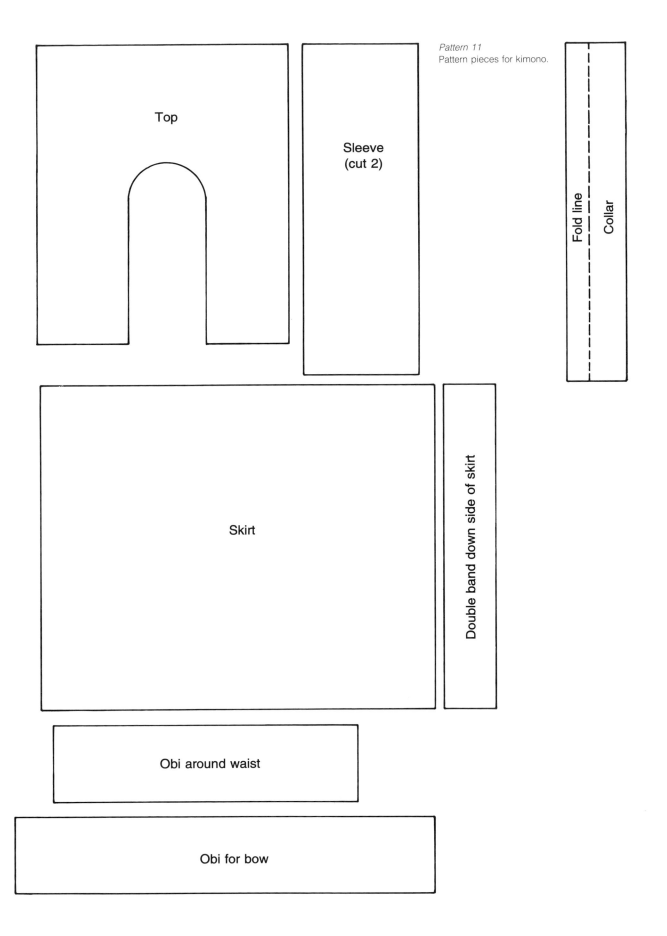

Top

Sleeve
(cut 2)

Fold line

Collar

Skirt

Double band down side of skirt

Obi around waist

Obi for bow

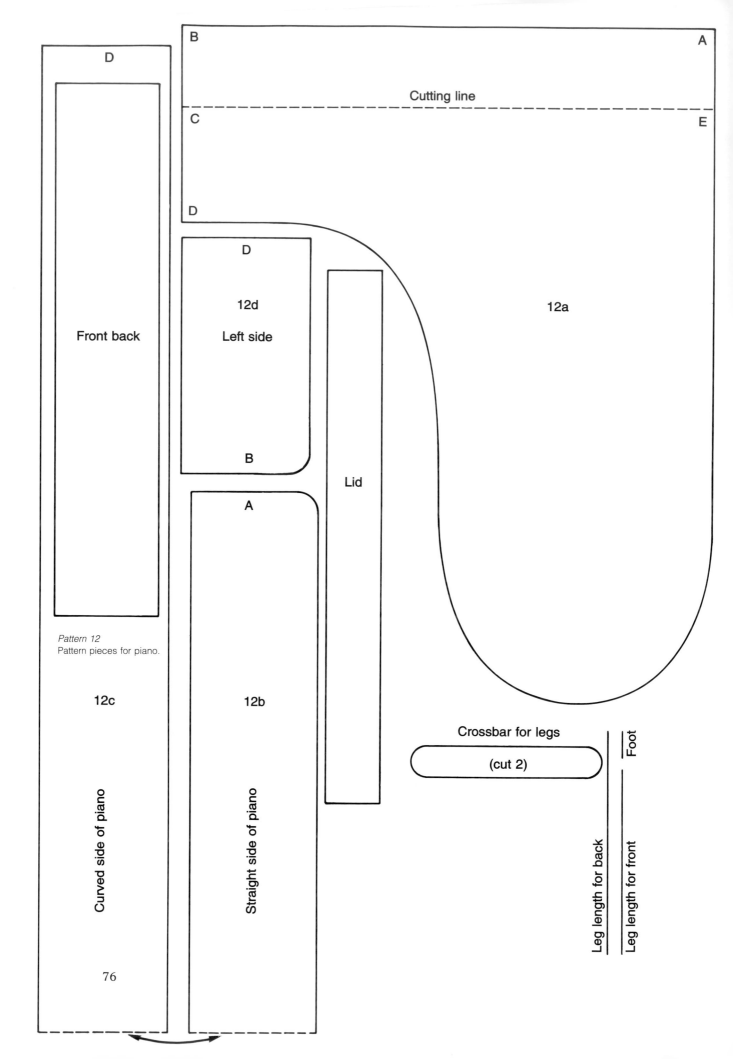

B

A

Cutting line

C

E

D

D

12d

Left side

B

A

12a

Lid

D

Front back

Pattern 12
Pattern pieces for piano.

12c

12b

Crossbar for legs

(cut 2)

Foot

Curved side of piano

Straight side of piano

Leg length for back

Leg length for front

76

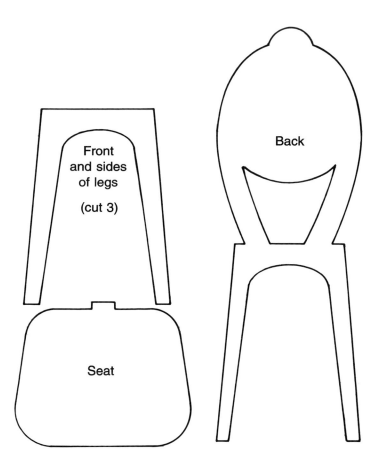

Front
and sides
of legs

(cut 3)

Back

Seat

Pattern 13
Pattern pieces for soiree
chairs.

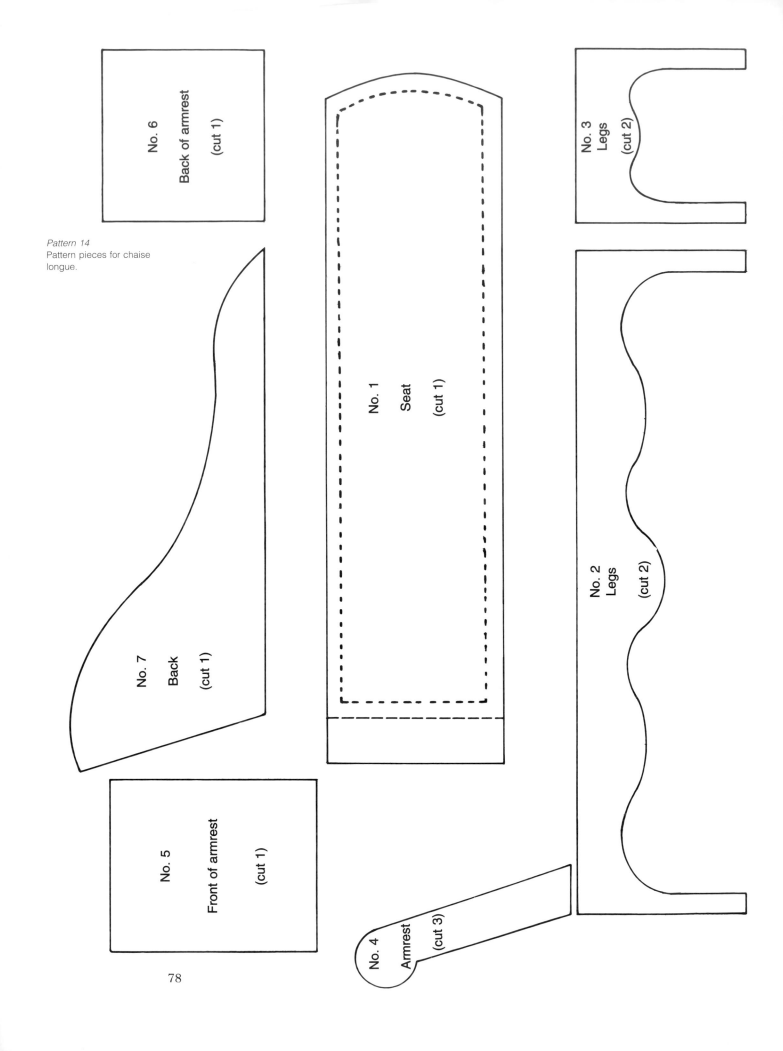

No. 6
Back of armrest
(cut 1)

No. 3
Legs
(cut 2)

Pattern 14
Pattern pieces for chaise
longue.

No. 7
Back
(cut 1)

No. 1
Seat
(cut 1)

No. 2
Legs
(cut 2)

No. 5
Front of armrest
(cut 1)

No. 4
Armrest
(cut 3)

78

Mirror
(cut 2)
Crossbar (cut 2)
Stand (cut 4)

Pattern 15
Pattern pieces for mirror.

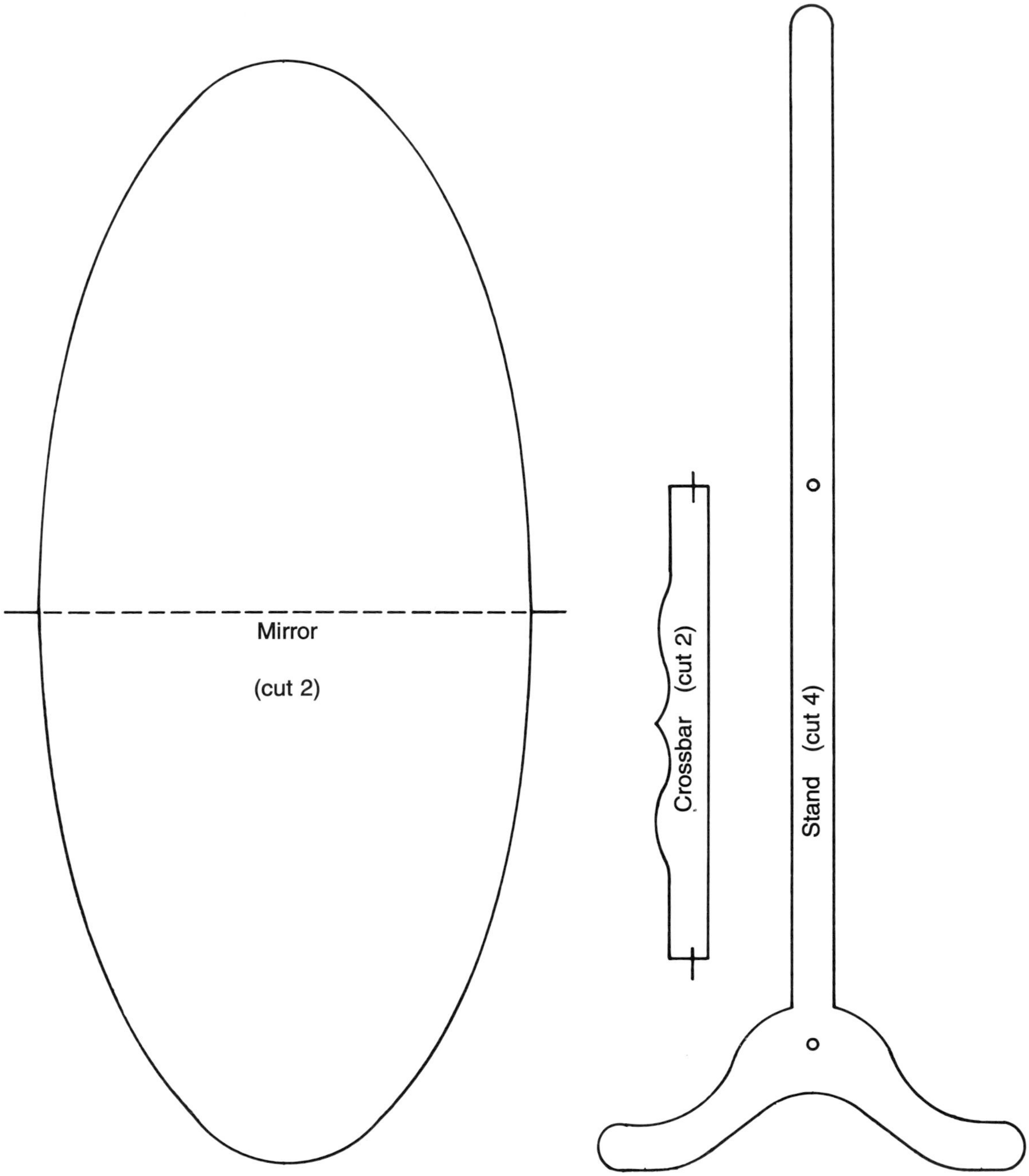

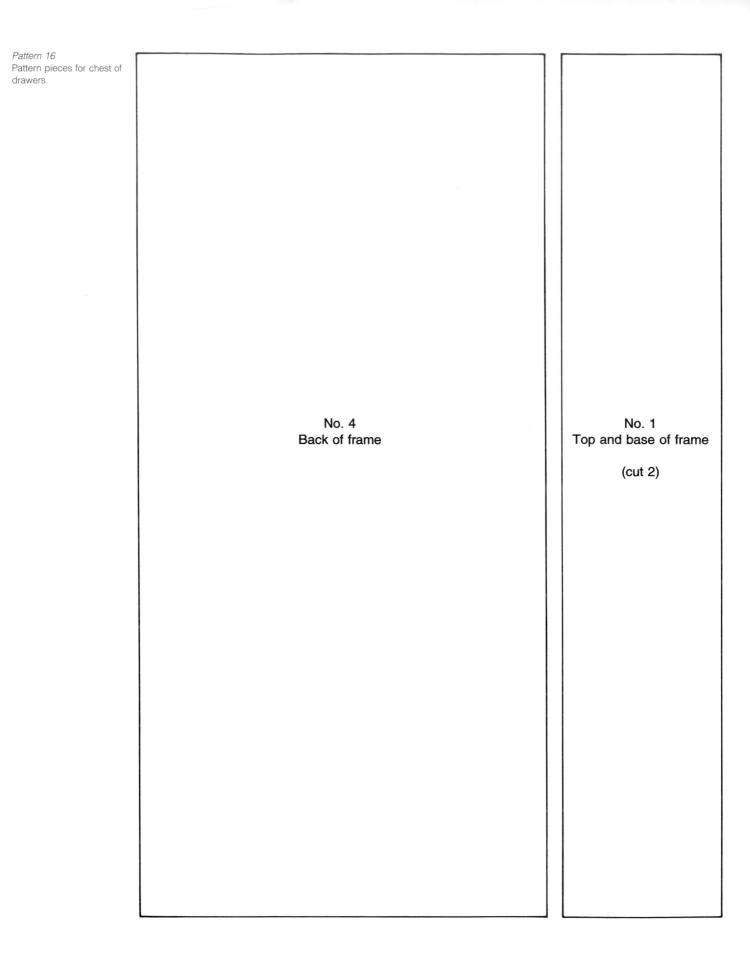

Pattern 16
Pattern pieces for chest of drawers.

No. 4
Back of frame

No. 1
Top and base of frame

(cut 2)

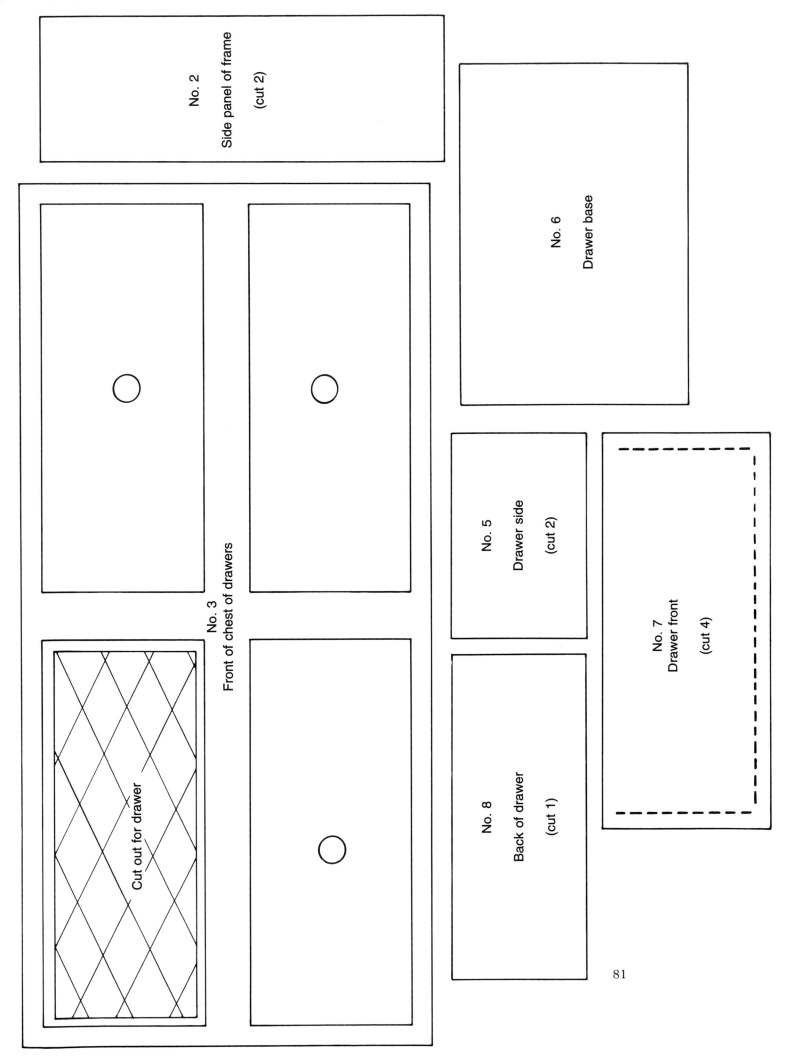

No. 2
Side panel of frame
(cut 2)

No. 6
Drawer base

No. 3
Front of chest of drawers

Cut out for drawer

No. 5
Drawer side
(cut 2)

No. 8
Back of drawer
(cut 1)

No. 7
Drawer front
(cut 4)

81

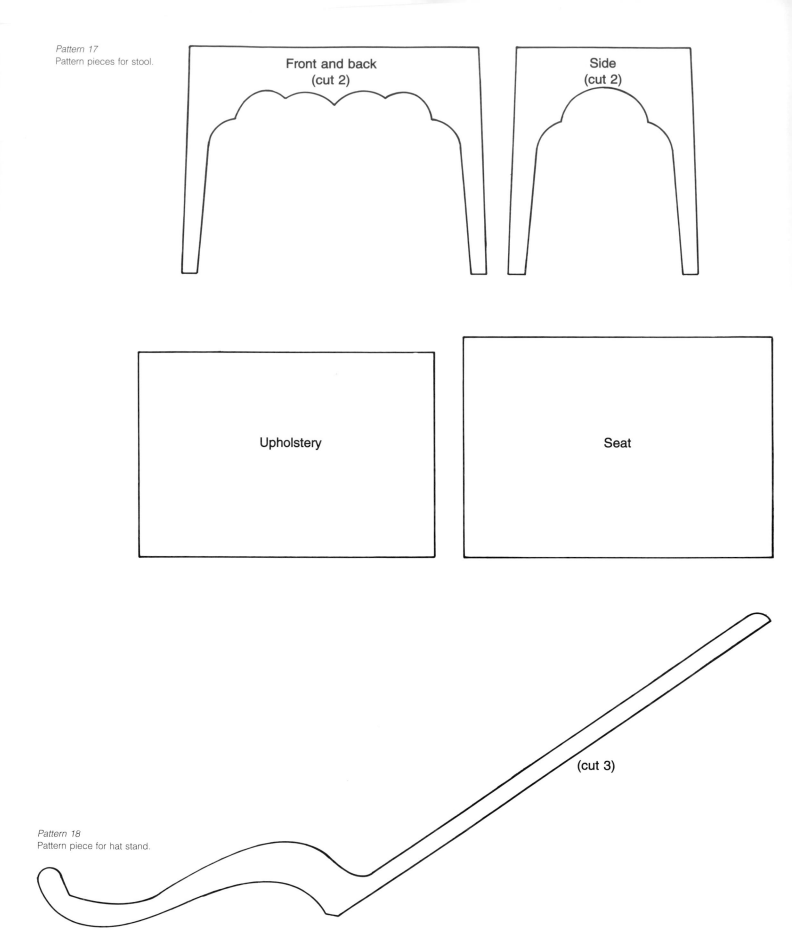

Front and back
(cut 2)

Side
(cut 2)

Upholstery

Seat

(cut 3)

Pattern 18
Pattern piece for hat stand.

82

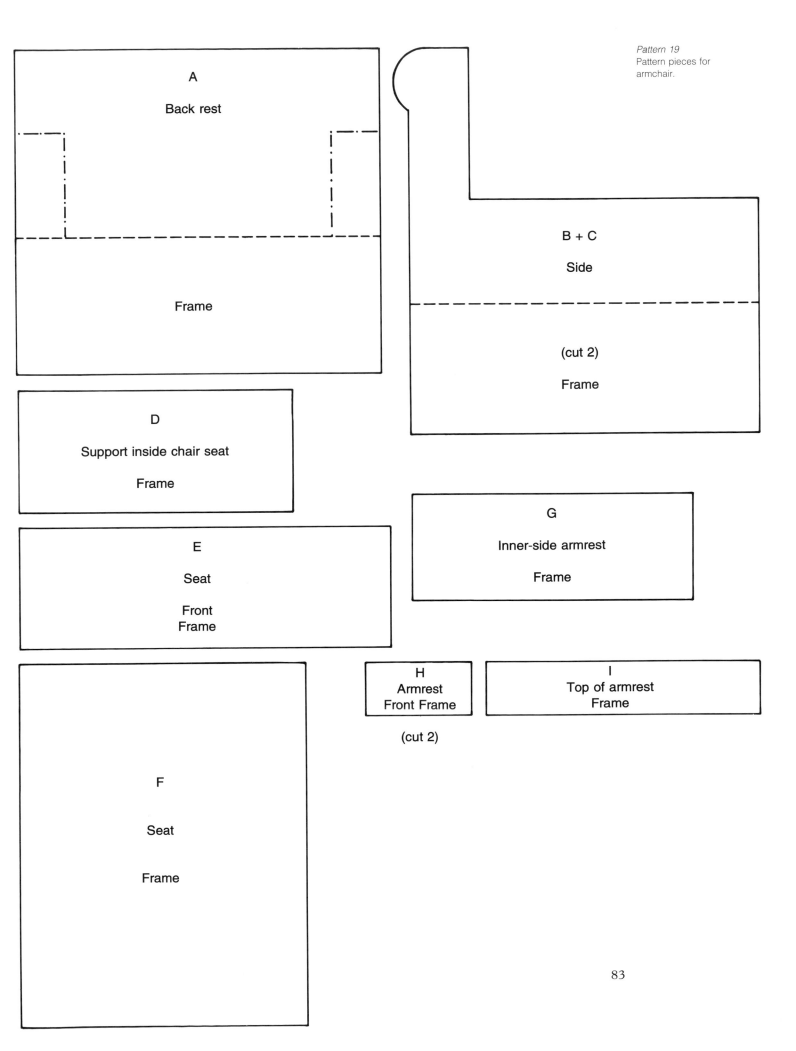

A

Back rest

Frame

B + C

Side

(cut 2)

Frame

D

Support inside chair seat

Frame

E

Seat

Front
Frame

G

Inner-side armrest

Frame

F

Seat

Frame

H
Armrest
Front Frame

(cut 2)

I
Top of armrest
Frame

Pattern 19
Pattern pieces for
armchair.

83

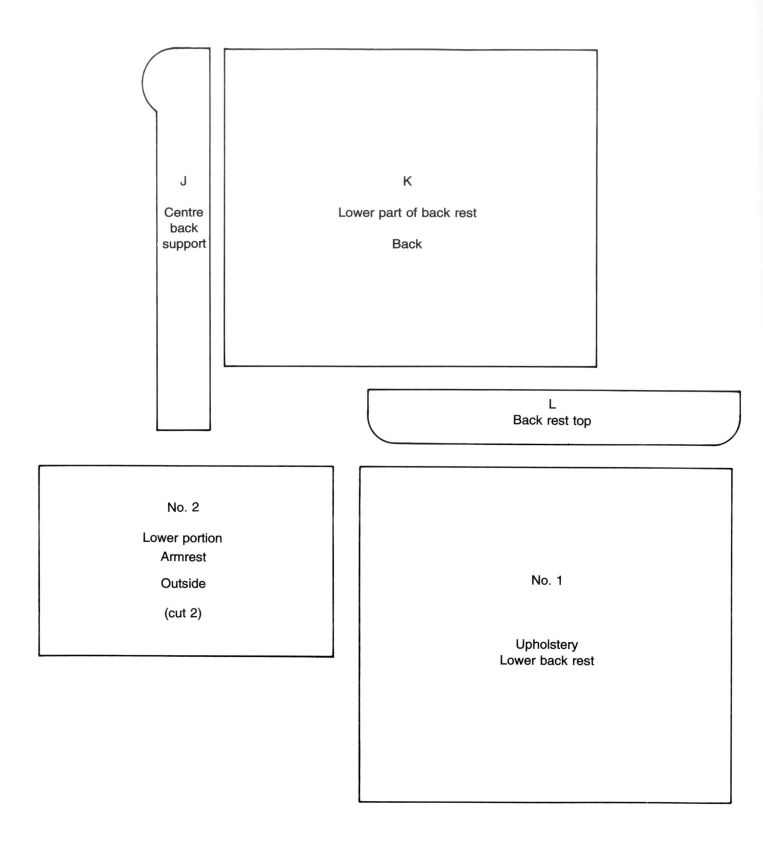

J

Centre
back
support

K

Lower part of back rest

Back

L
Back rest top

No. 2

Lower portion
Armrest

Outside

(cut 2)

No. 1

Upholstery
Lower back rest

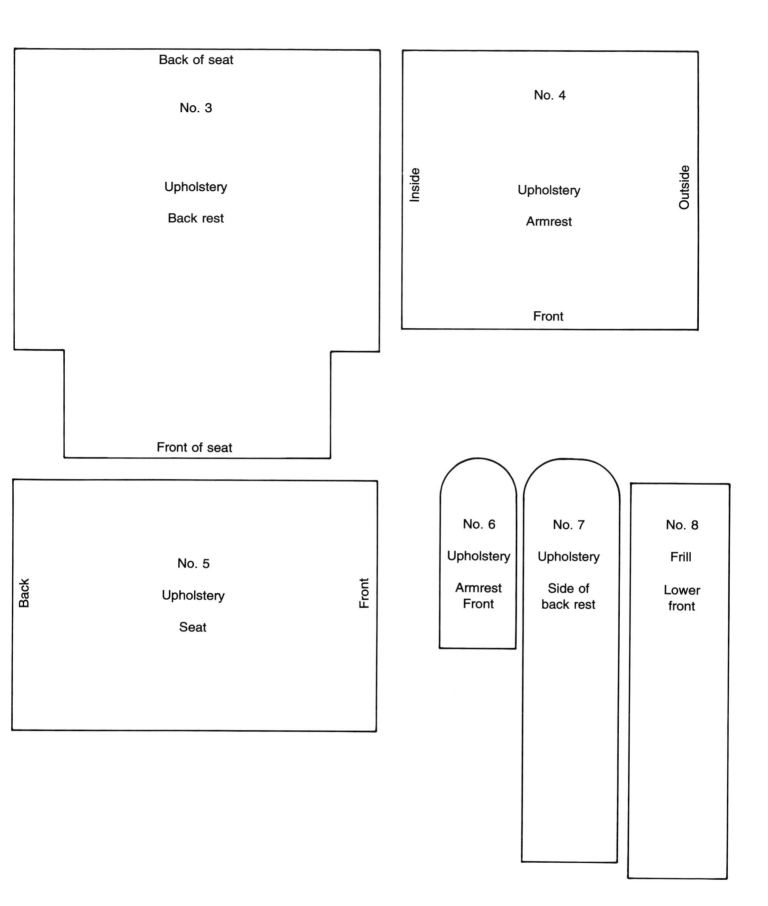

Back of seat

No. 3

Upholstery

Back rest

Front of seat

No. 4

Inside

Outside

Upholstery

Armrest

Front

No. 5

Upholstery

Seat

Back

Front

No. 6

Upholstery

Armrest
Front

No. 7

Upholstery

Side of
back rest

No. 8

Frill

Lower
front

Pattern 20
Pattern pieces for upright
chair.

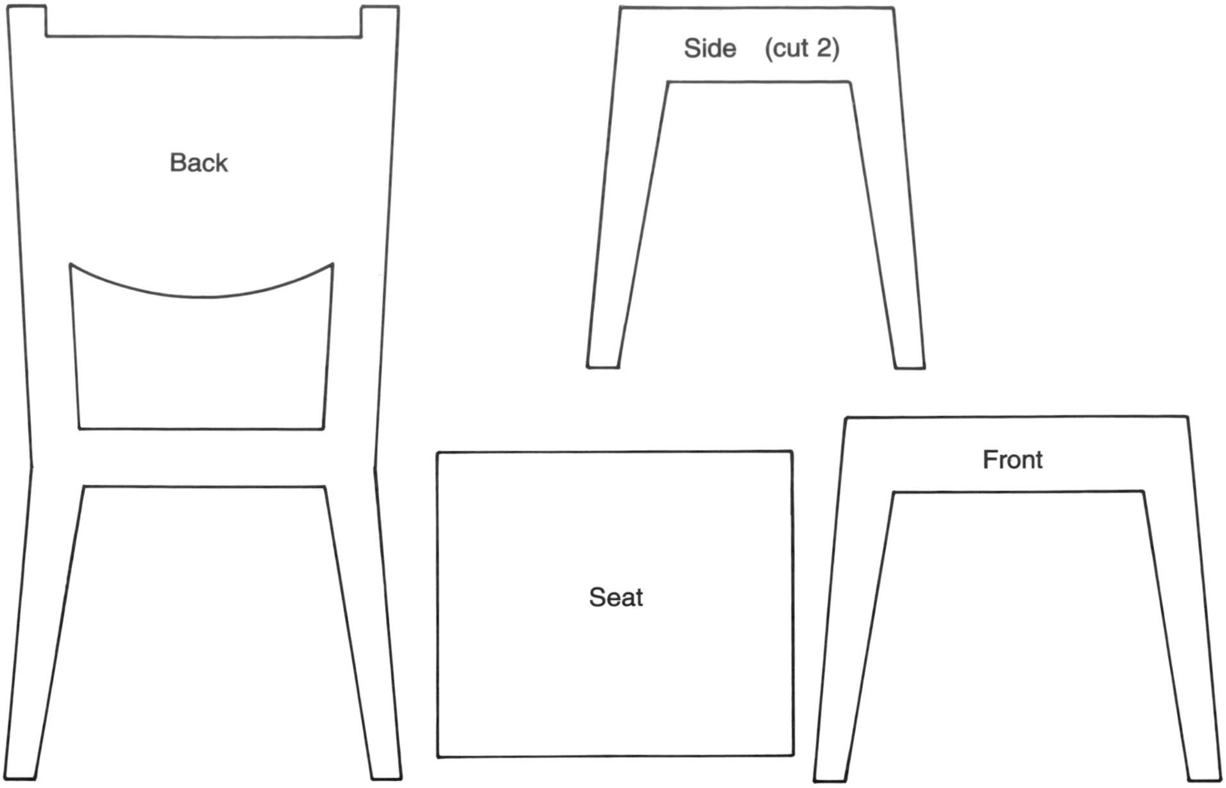

Back

Side   (cut 2)

Front

Seat

Wheels
(cut 2)

Wheels
(cut 2)

Pattern 21
Pattern pieces for pram.

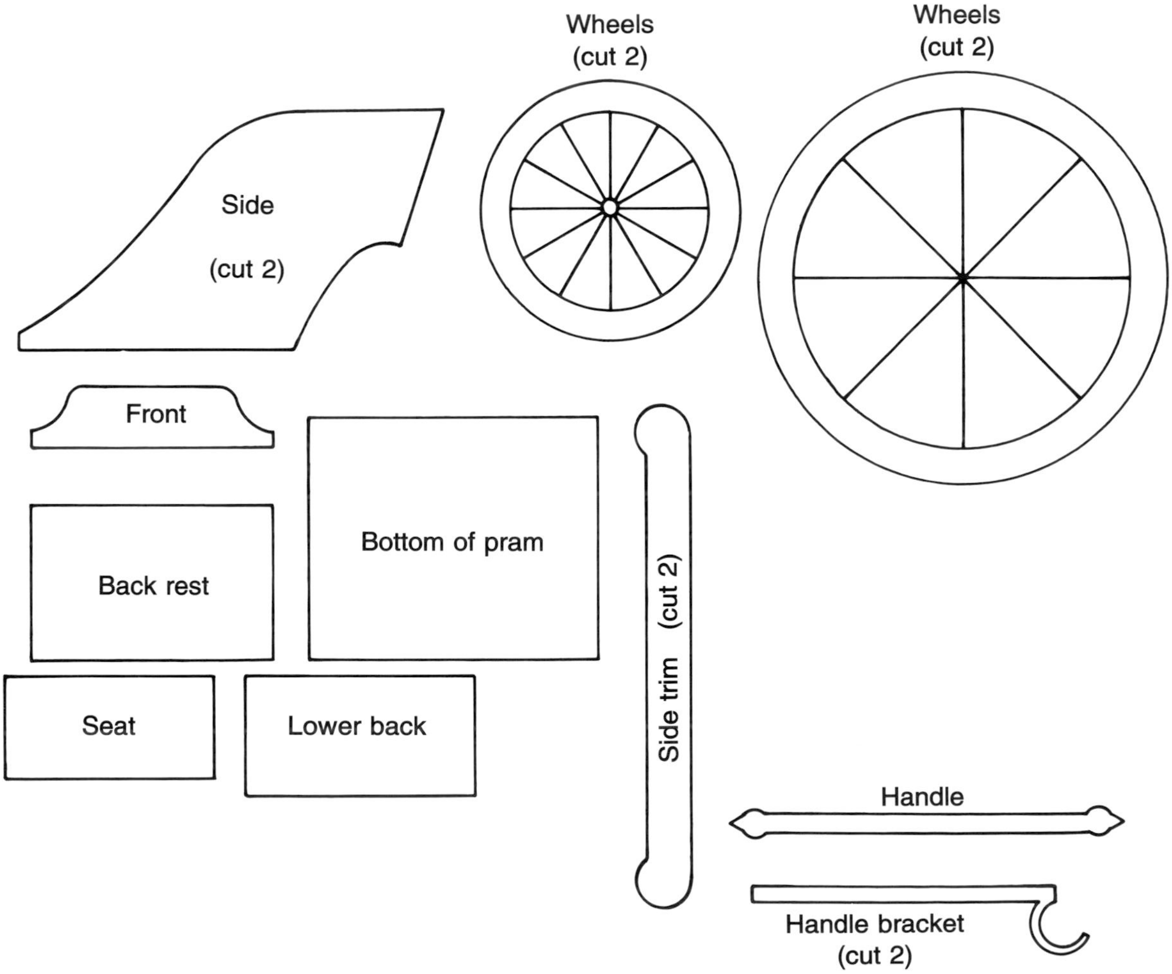

Side

(cut 2)

Front

Bottom of pram

Back rest

Side trim   (cut 2)

Seat

Lower back

Handle

Handle bracket
(cut 2)

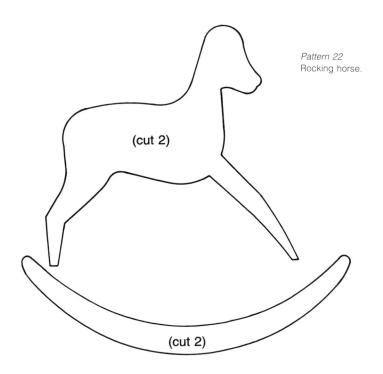

Pattern 22
Rocking horse.

(cut 2)

(cut 2)

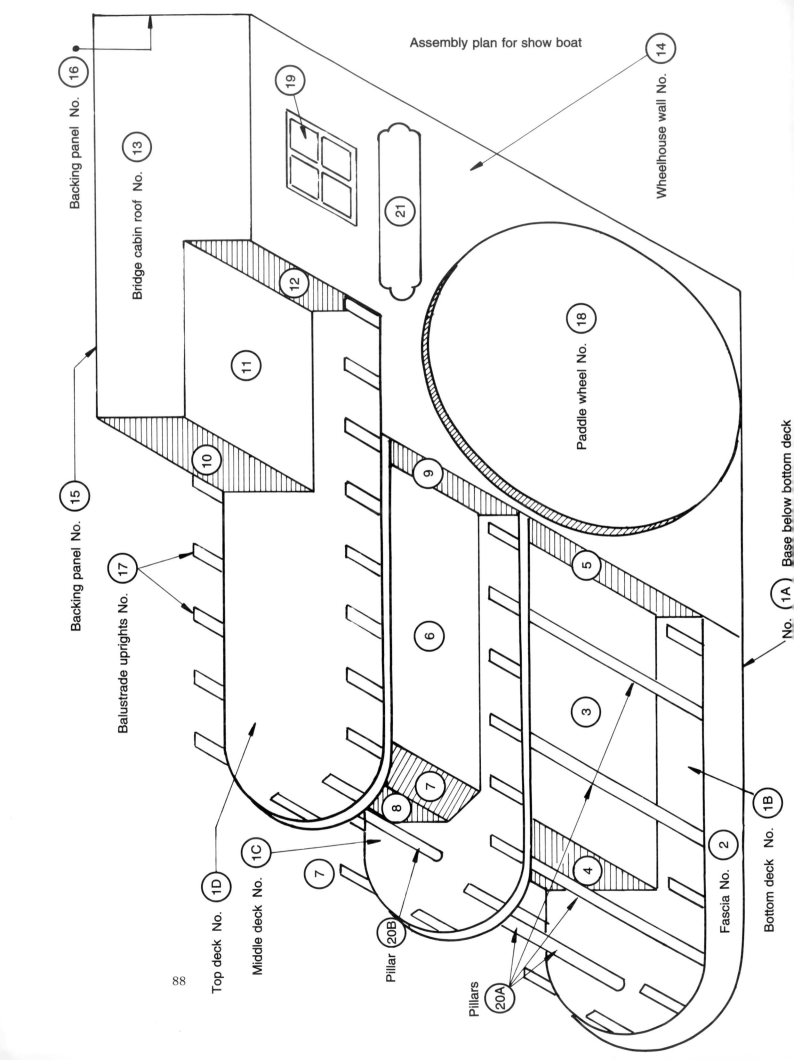

Assembly plan for show boat

Backing panel No. (16)

Bridge cabin roof No. (13)

Backing panel No. (15)

Balustrade uprights No. (17)

Wheelhouse wall No. (14)

Paddle wheel No. (18)

Top deck No. (1D)

Middle deck No. (1C)

Pillar (20B)

Pillars
(20A)

Fascia No. (2)

Bottom deck No. (1B)

No. (1A) Base below bottom deck

(19)

(21)

(12)

(11)

(10)

(9)

(8)

(7)

(6)

(5)

(4)

(3)

(7)

88

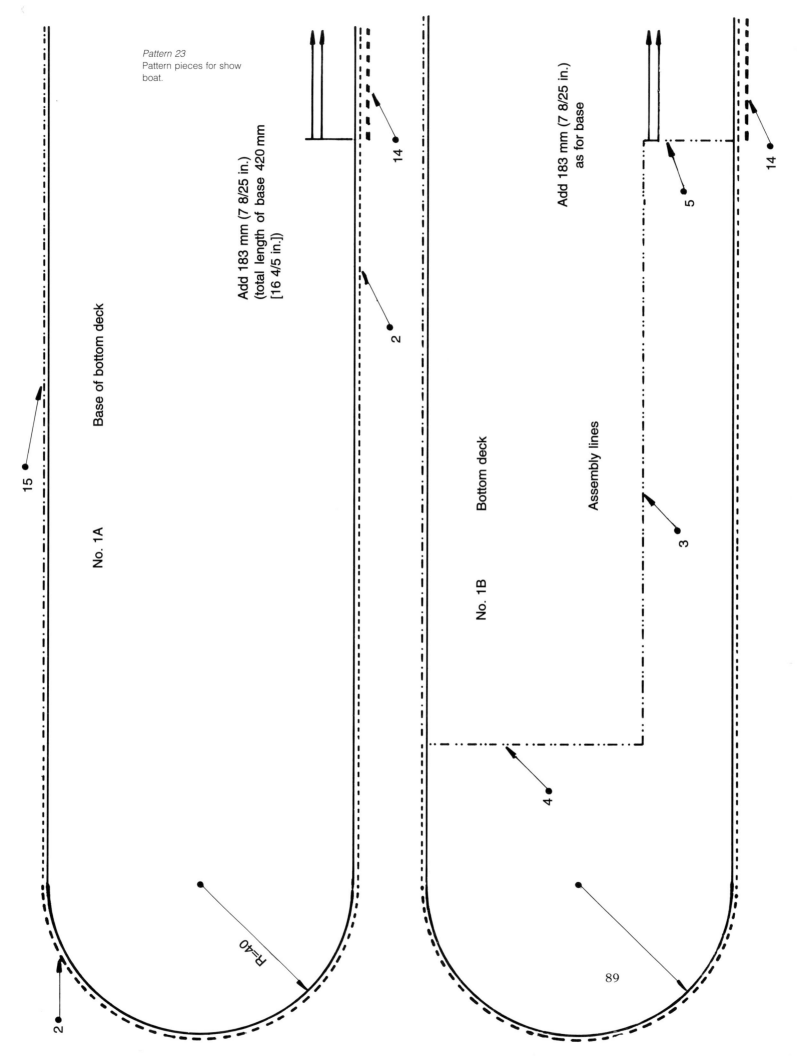

Pattern 23
Pattern pieces for show boat.

Base of bottom deck

No. 1A

15

2

2

14

Add 183 mm (7 8/25 in.) (total length of base 420 mm [16 4/5 in.])

R=40

Bottom deck

No. 1B

Assembly lines

3

4

5

14

Add 183 mm (7 8/25 in.) as for base

89

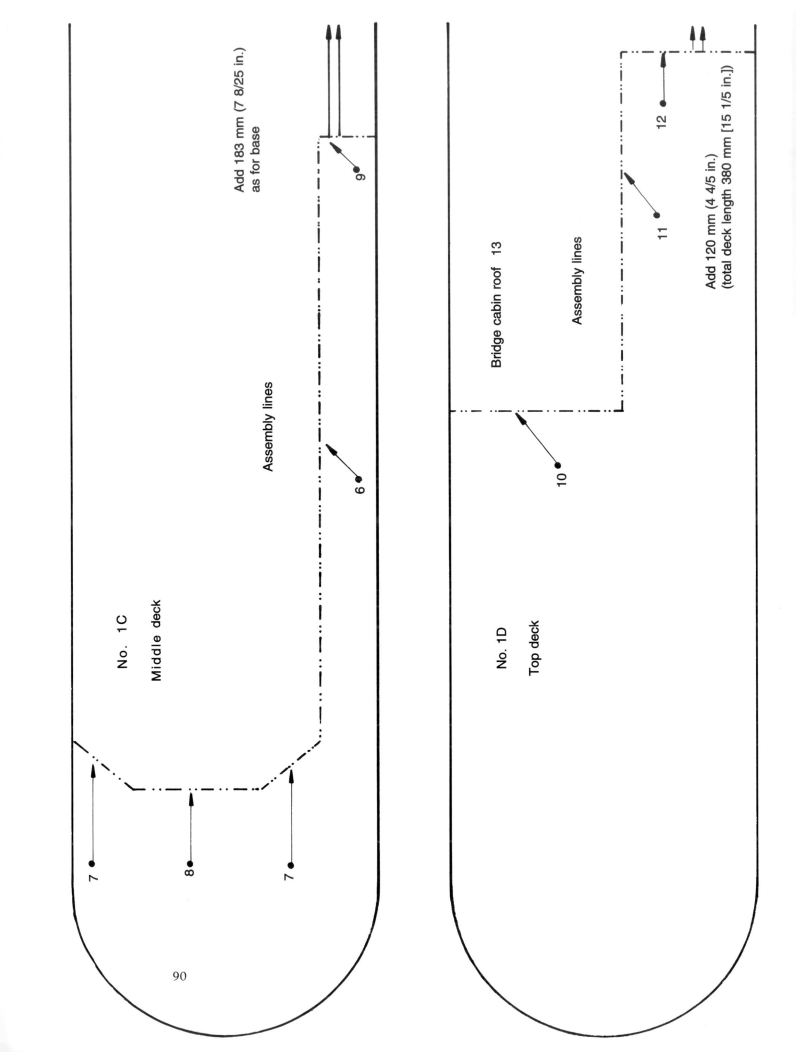

Add 183 mm (7 8/25 in.)
as for base

Assembly lines

9

No. 1C

Middle deck

7

8

7

90

Add 120 mm (4 4/5 in.)
(total deck length 380 mm [15 1/5 in.])

12

11

Bridge cabin roof 13

Assembly lines

10

No. 1D

Top deck

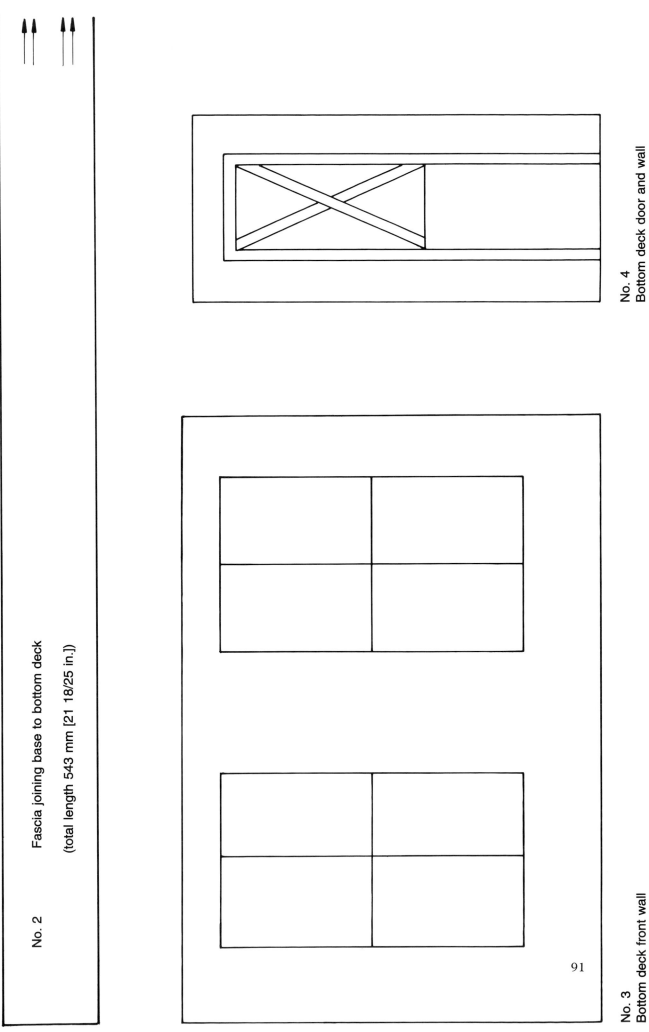

No. 2 Fascia joining base to bottom deck

(total length 543 mm [21 18/25 in.])

No. 3
Bottom deck front wall

No. 4
Bottom deck door and wall

91

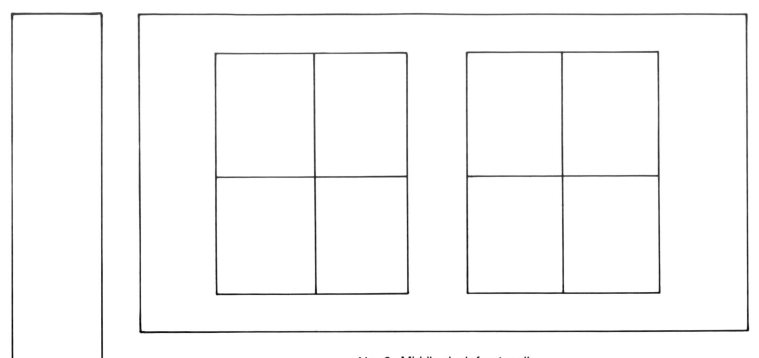

No. 6 Middle deck front wall

No. 5 Bottom deck wall

No. 7 Middle deck bell wall and rear wall   (cut 2)

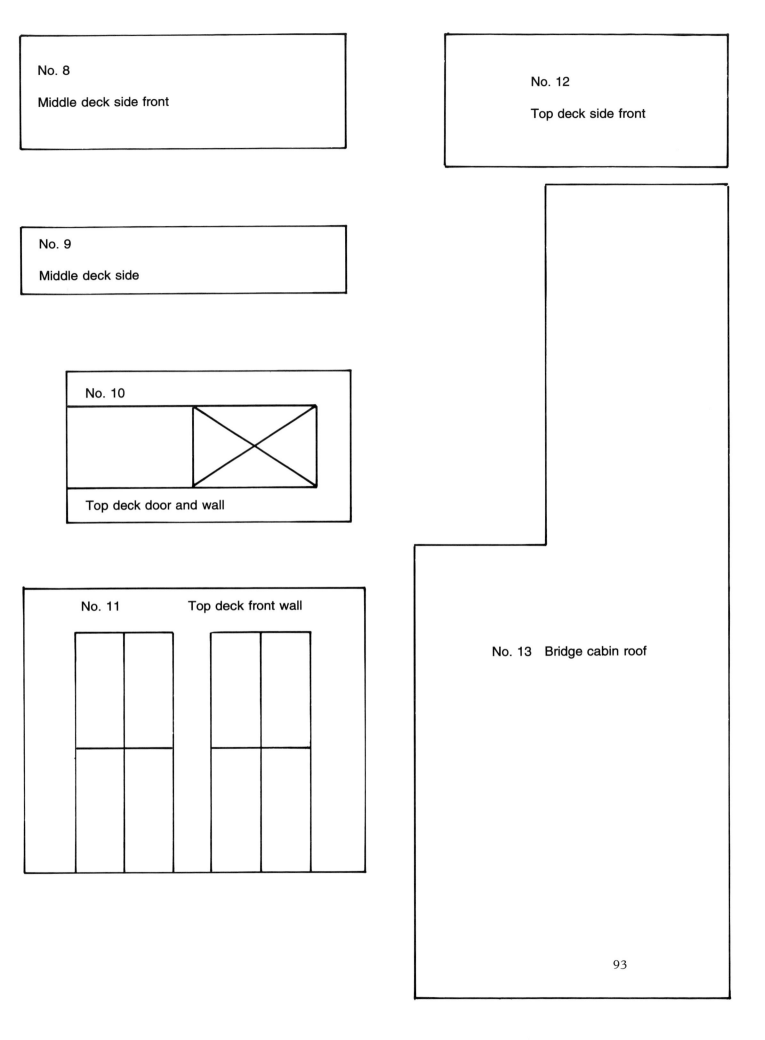

No. 8

Middle deck side front

No. 9

Middle deck side

No. 10

Top deck door and wall

No. 11   Top deck front wall

No. 12

Top deck side front

No. 13   Bridge cabin roof

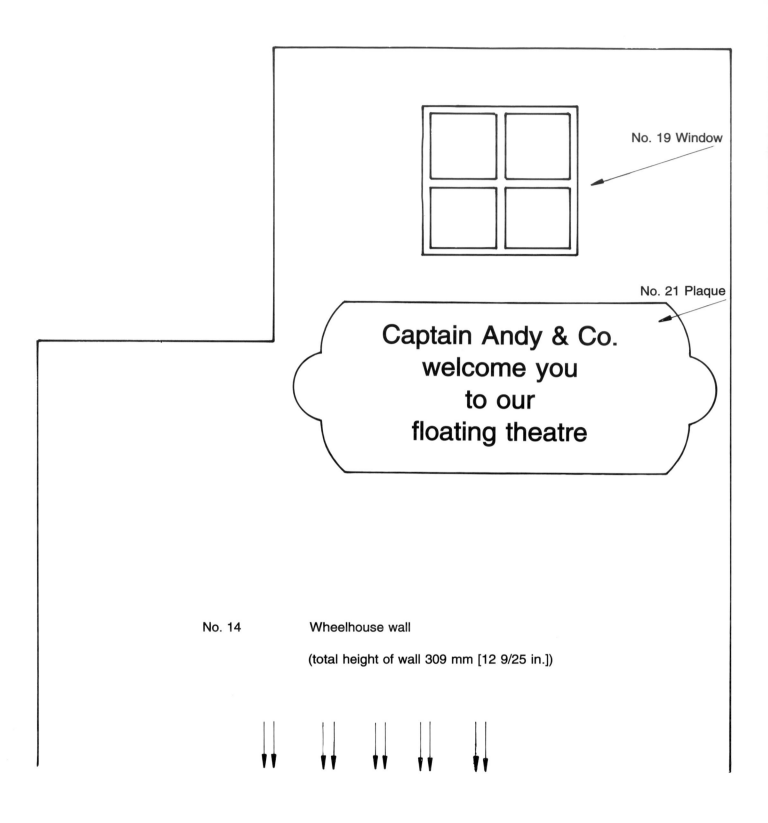

No. 19 Window

No. 21 Plaque

**Captain Andy & Co.
welcome you
to our
floating theatre**

No. 14   Wheelhouse wall

(total height of wall 309 mm [12 9/25 in.])

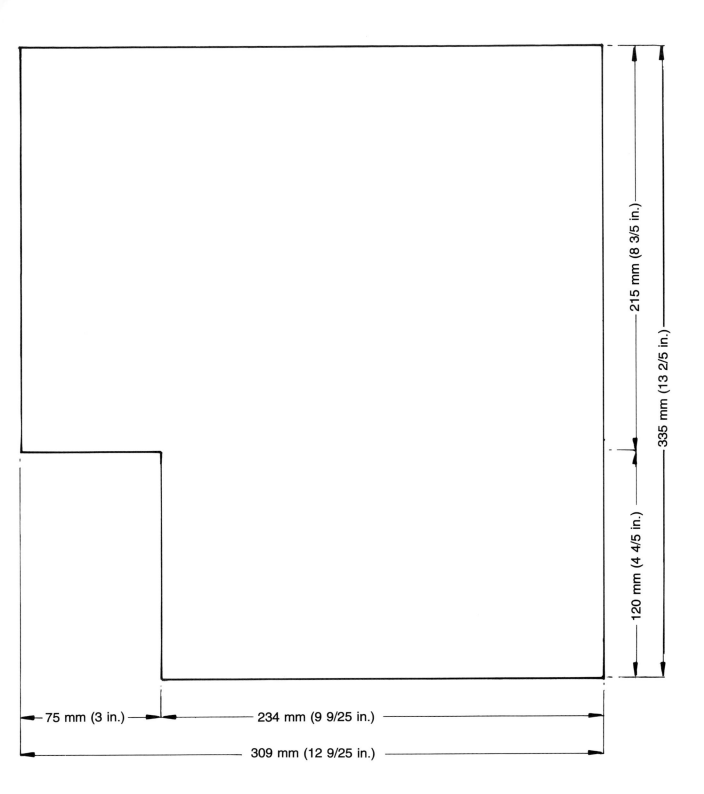

215 mm (8 3/5 in.)

335 mm (13 2/5 in.)

120 mm (4 4/5 in.)

75 mm (3 in.)

234 mm (9 9/25 in.)

309 mm (12 9/25 in.)

No. 15   Backing panel

(Pattern has been drawn half size –

to make, work to dimensions shown)

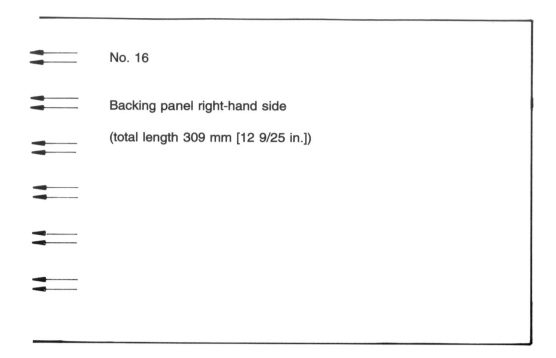

No. 16

Backing panel right-hand side

(total length 309 mm [12 9/25 in.])

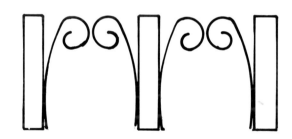

No. 17   Balustrades

(cut 34 uprights)

(cut 68 trimmings)

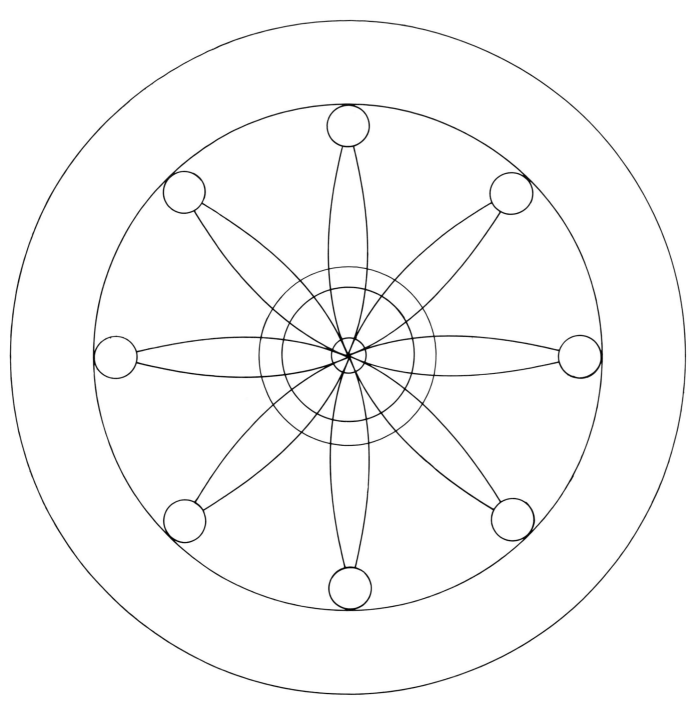

No. 18   Paddle wheel

No. 20A

Bottom deck pillars

(cut 5)

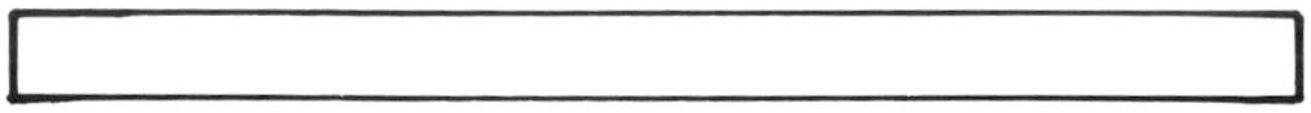

No. 20B

Middle deck pillar

(cut 1)

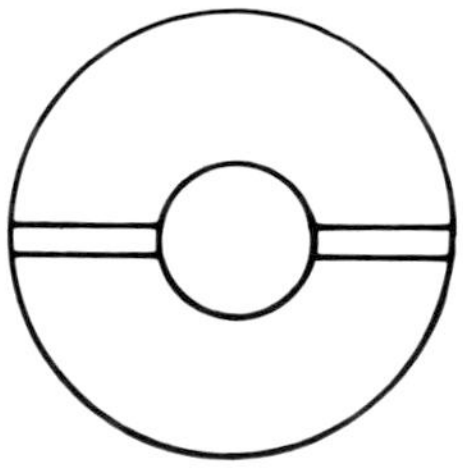

No. 22

Life belt

COTTON BLOSSOM

Pattern 24
Key to the pattern pieces
of The Victorian house.

KEY PLAN

99

1

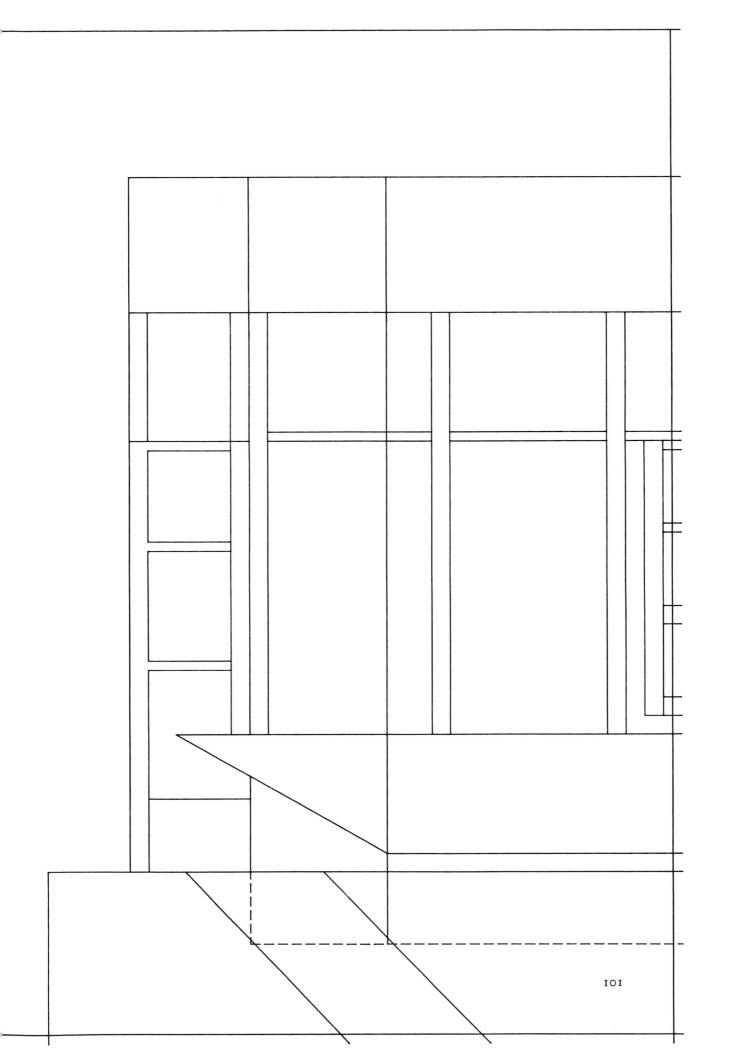

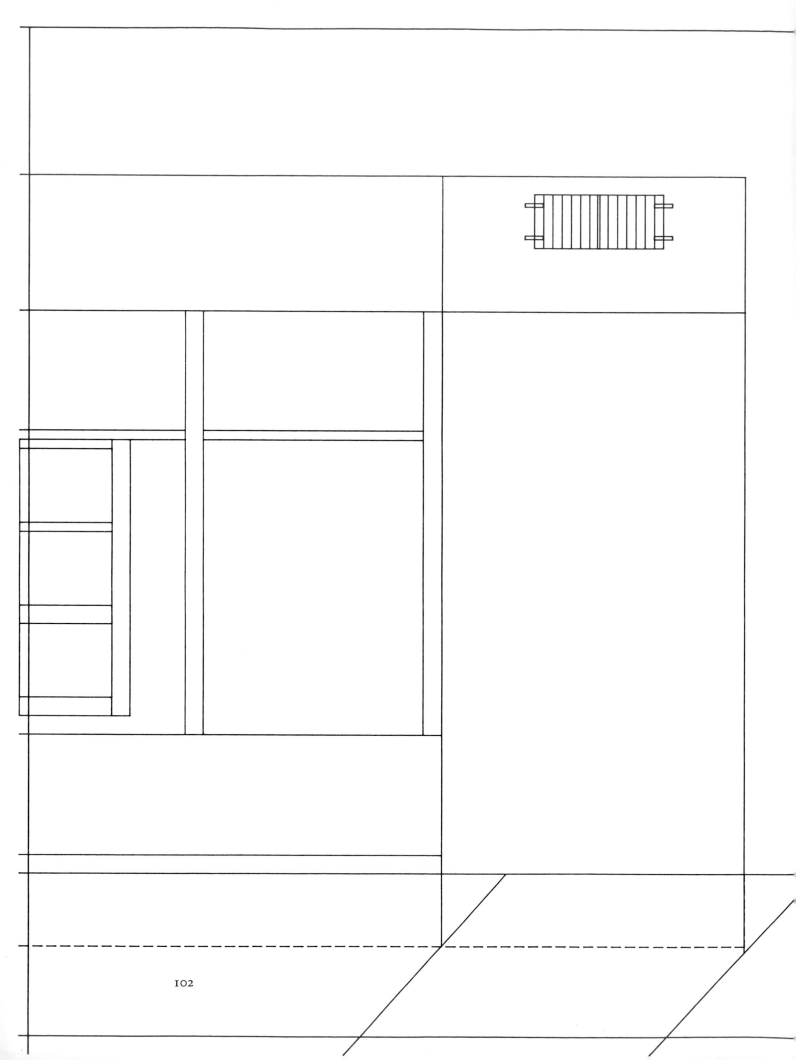

2

3

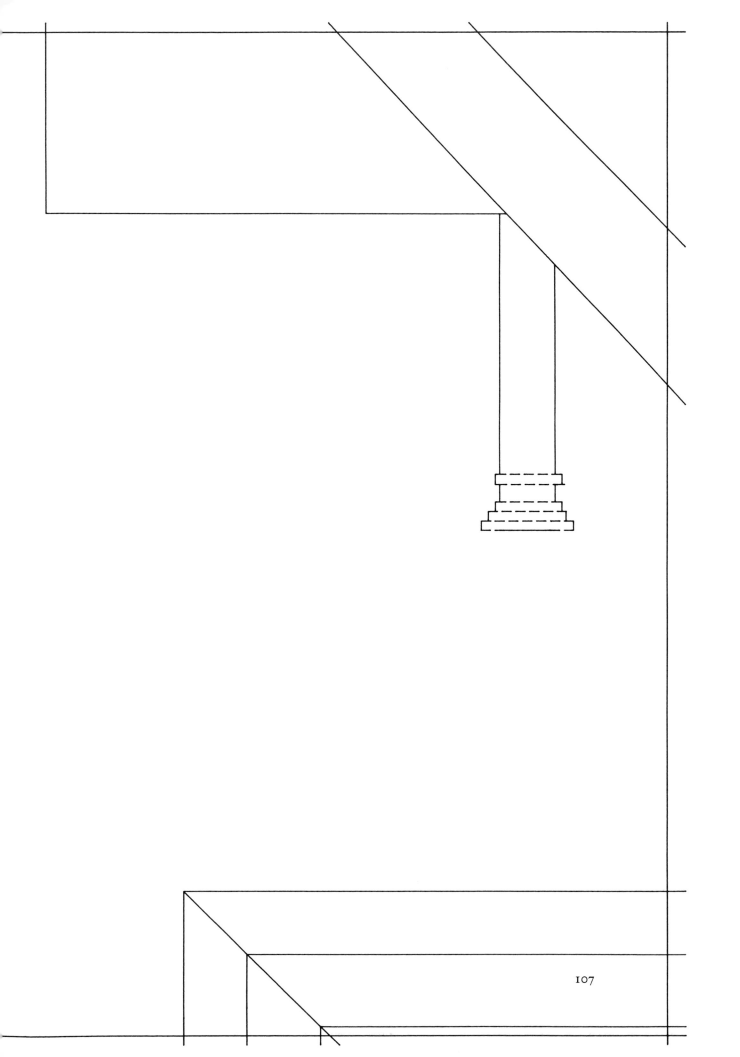

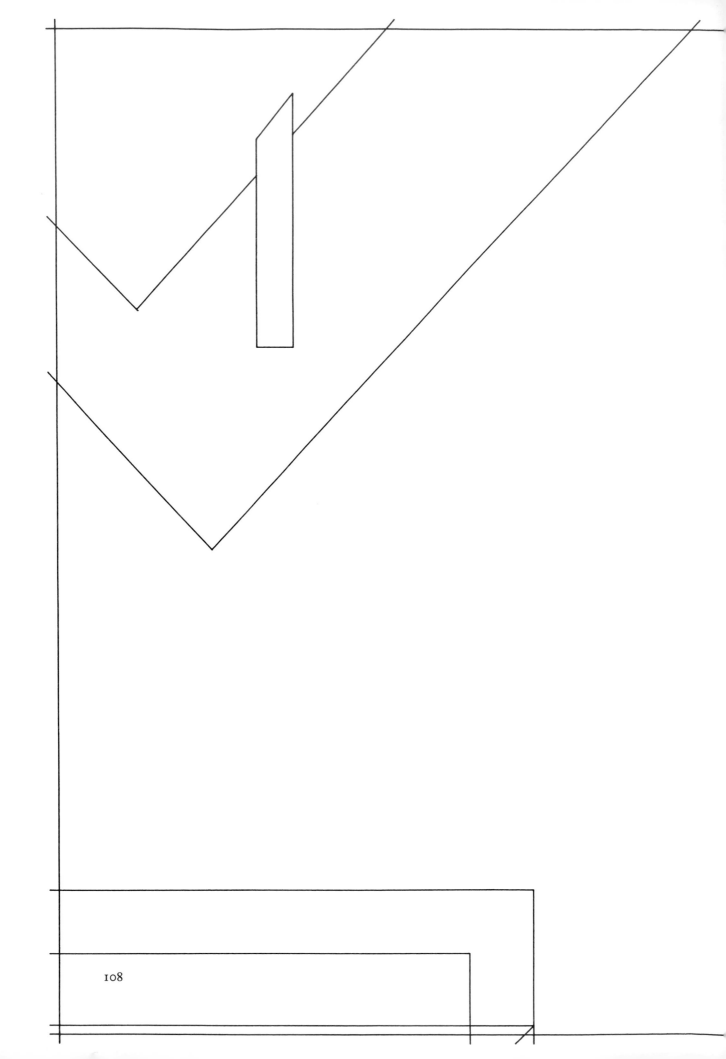

5

6

7

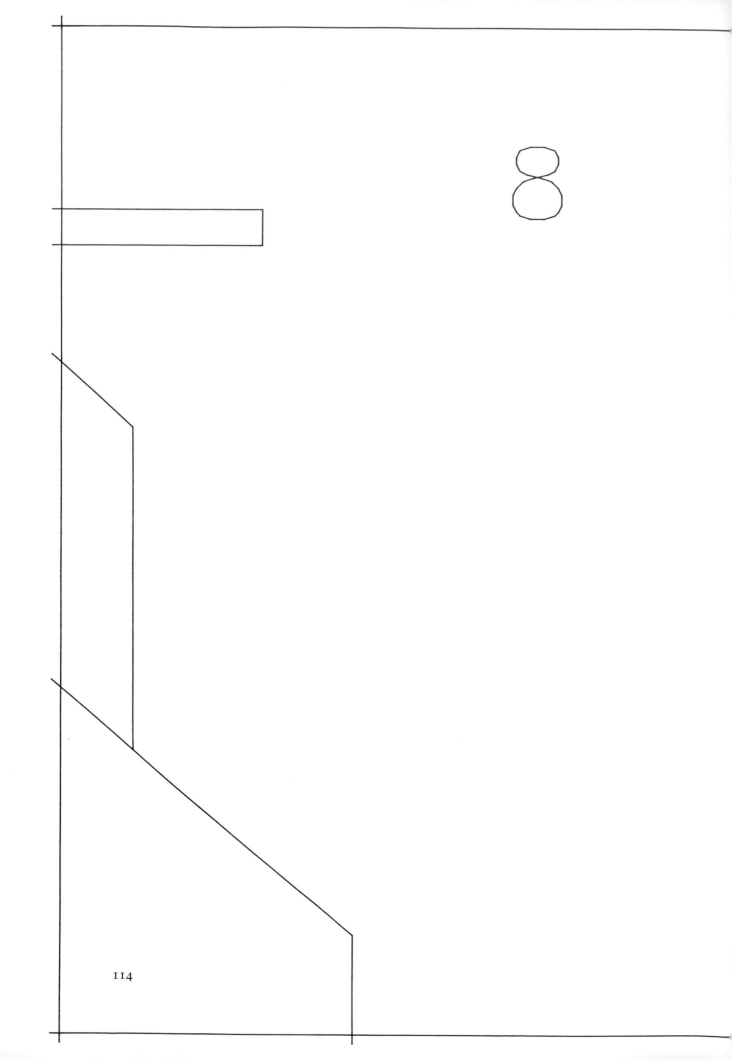

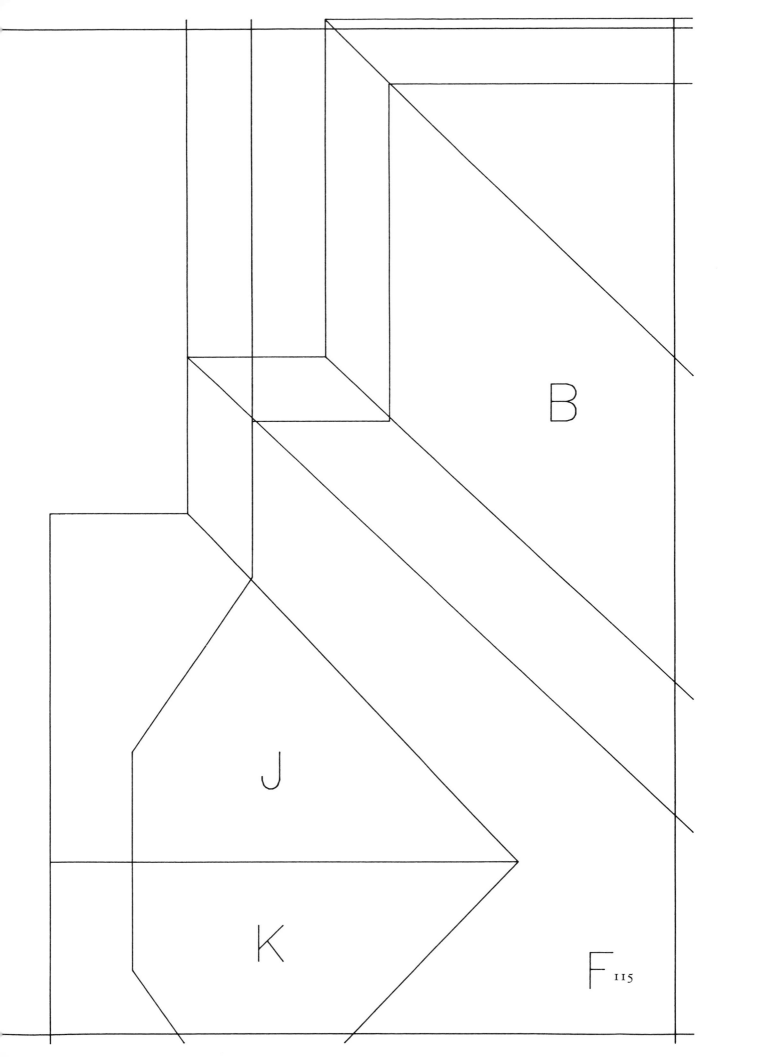

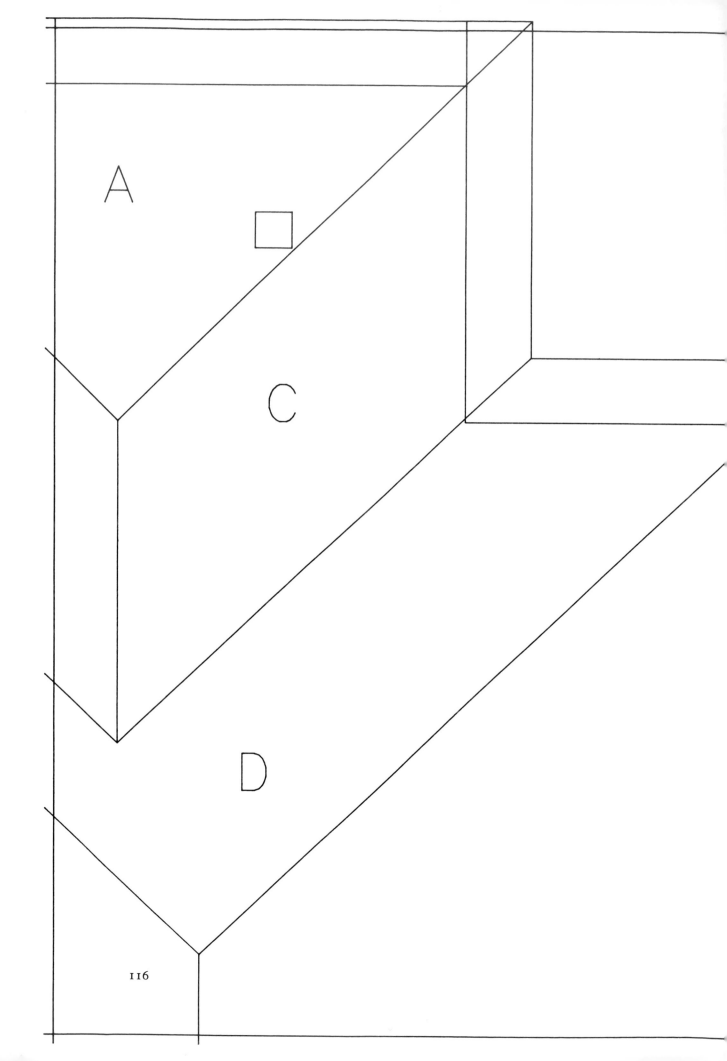

A

C

D

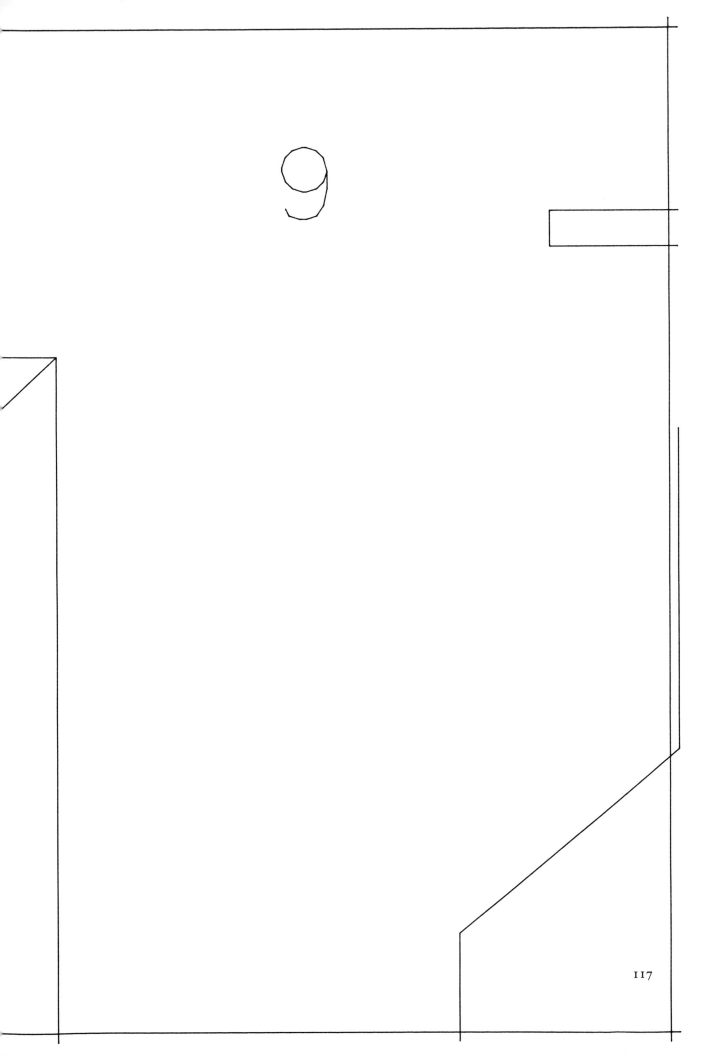

9

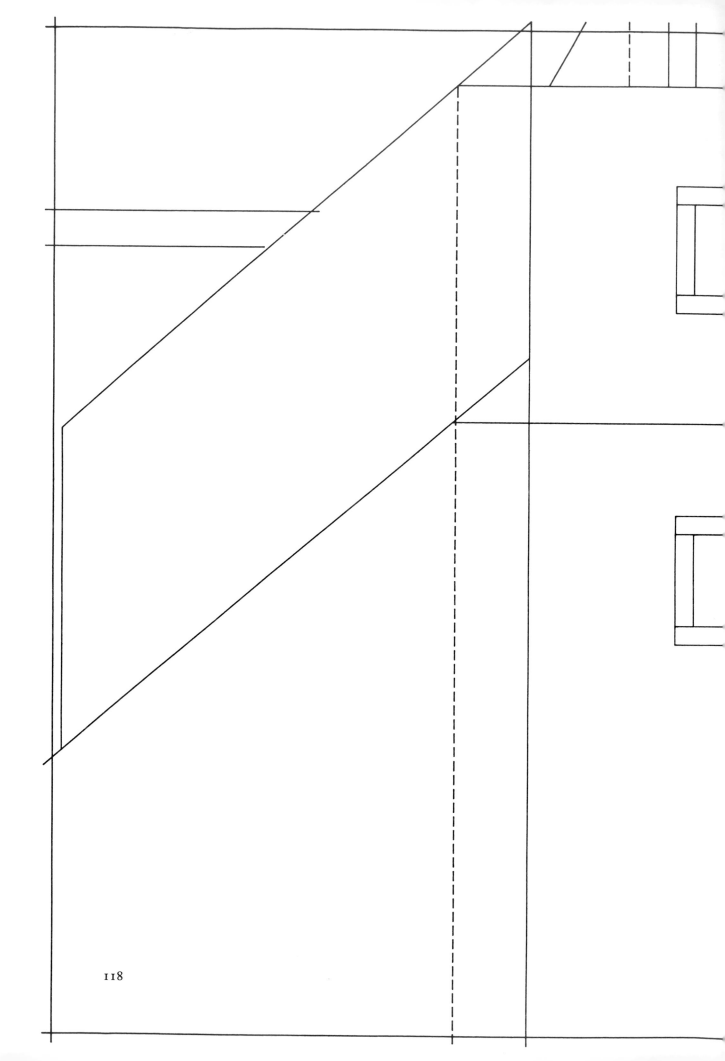

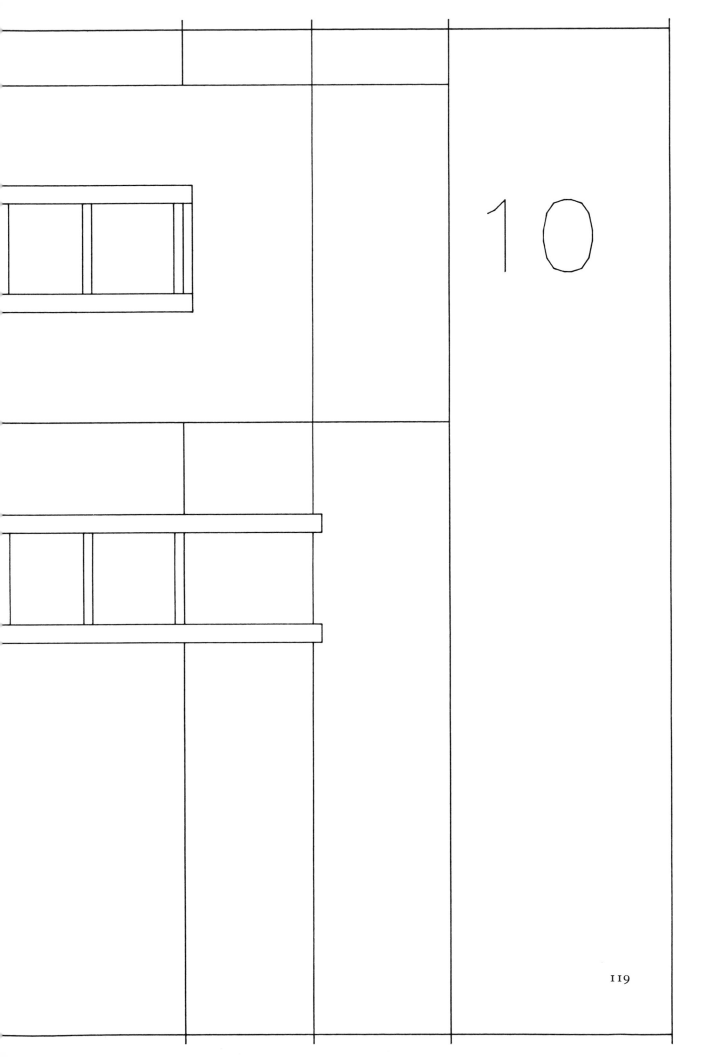

10

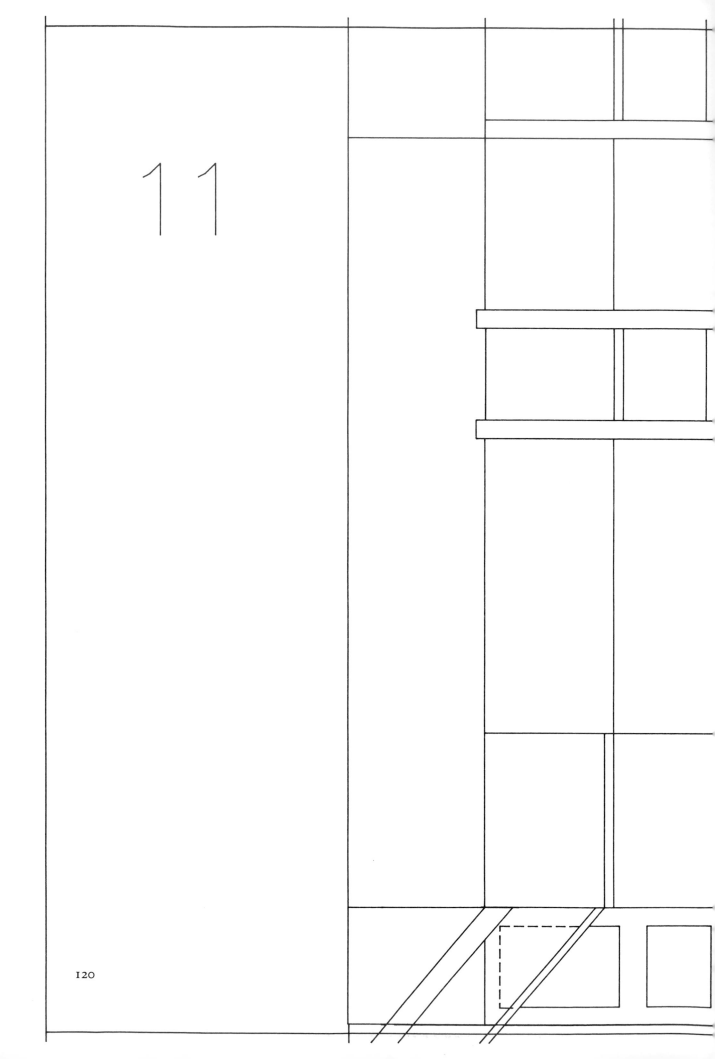

11

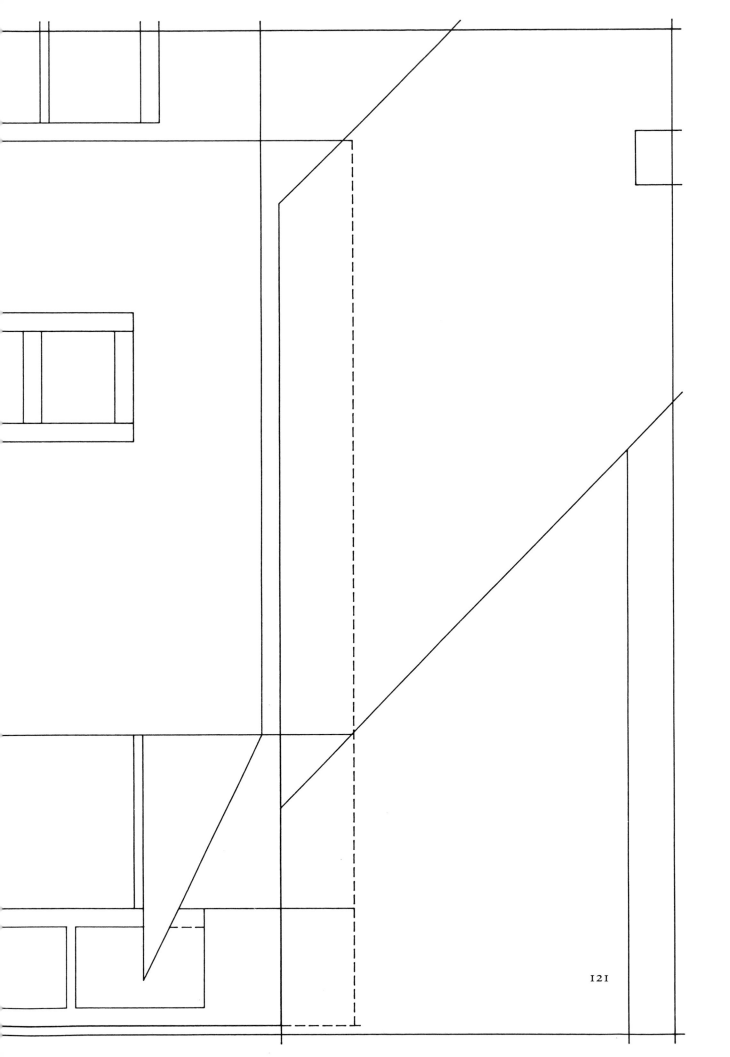

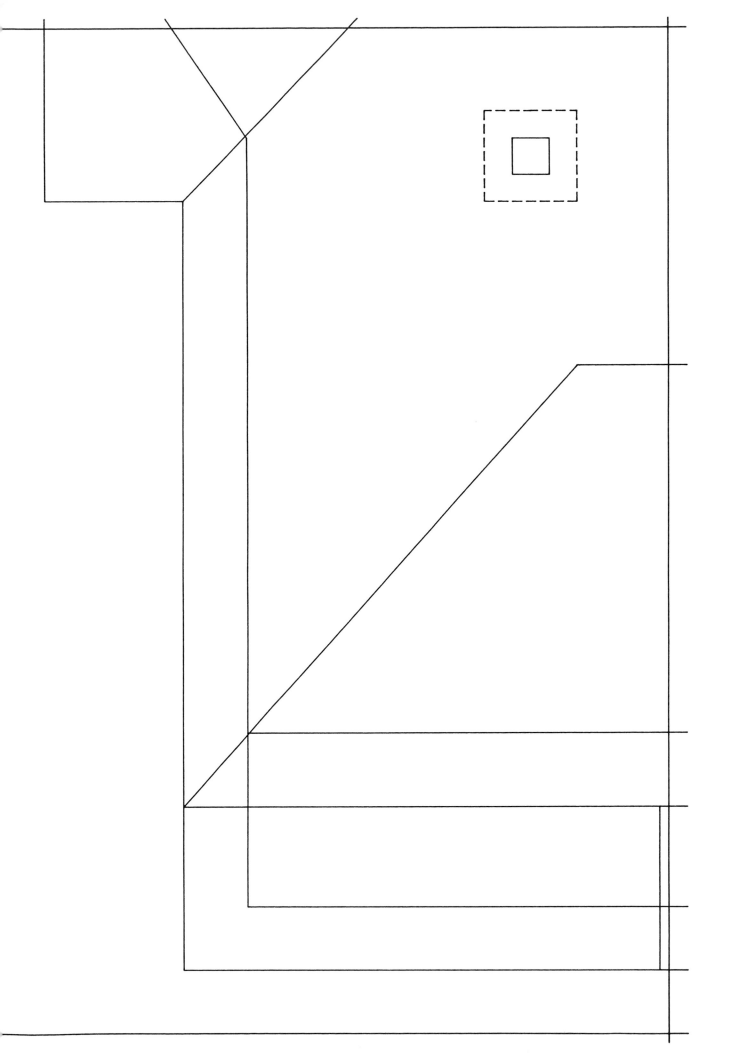

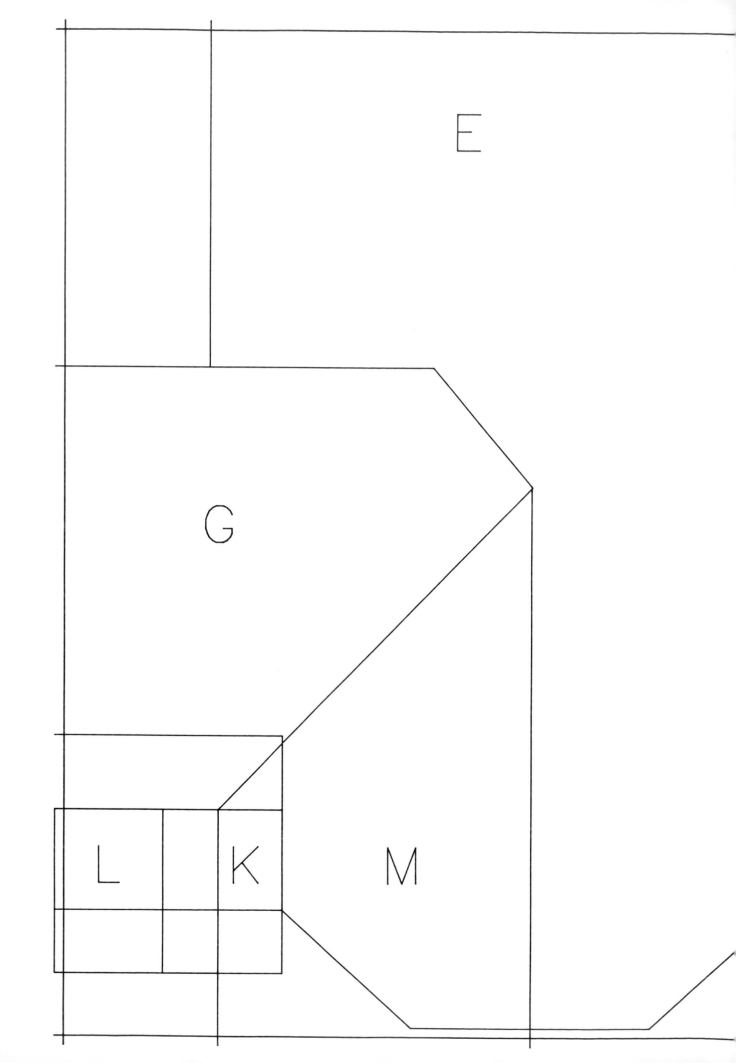

13

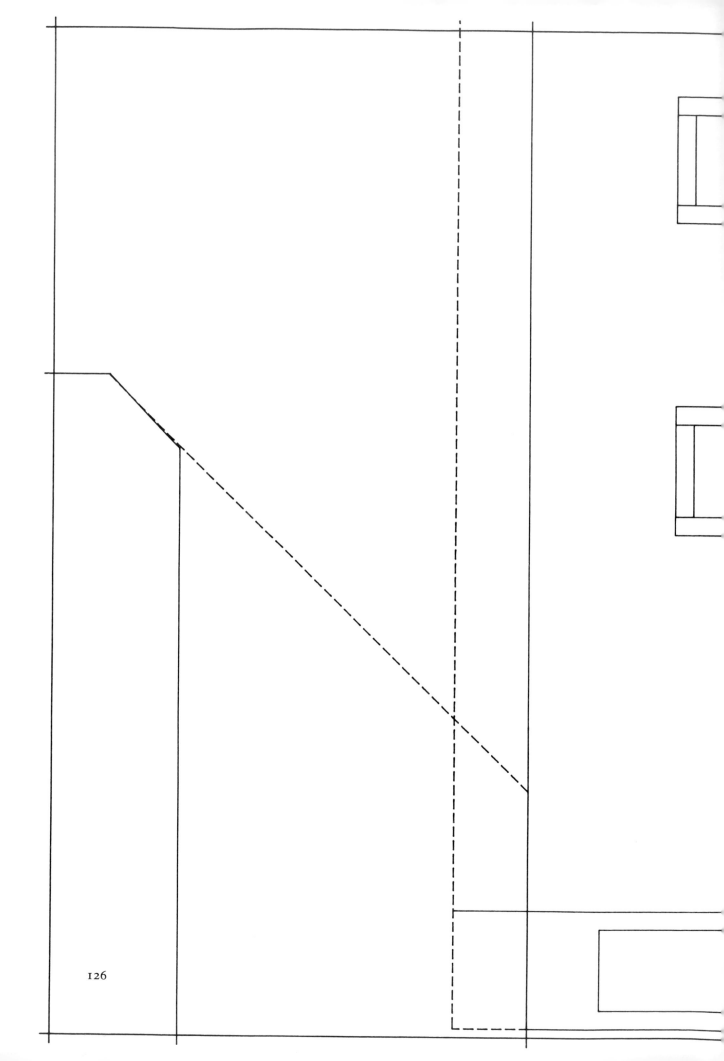

14

15

16

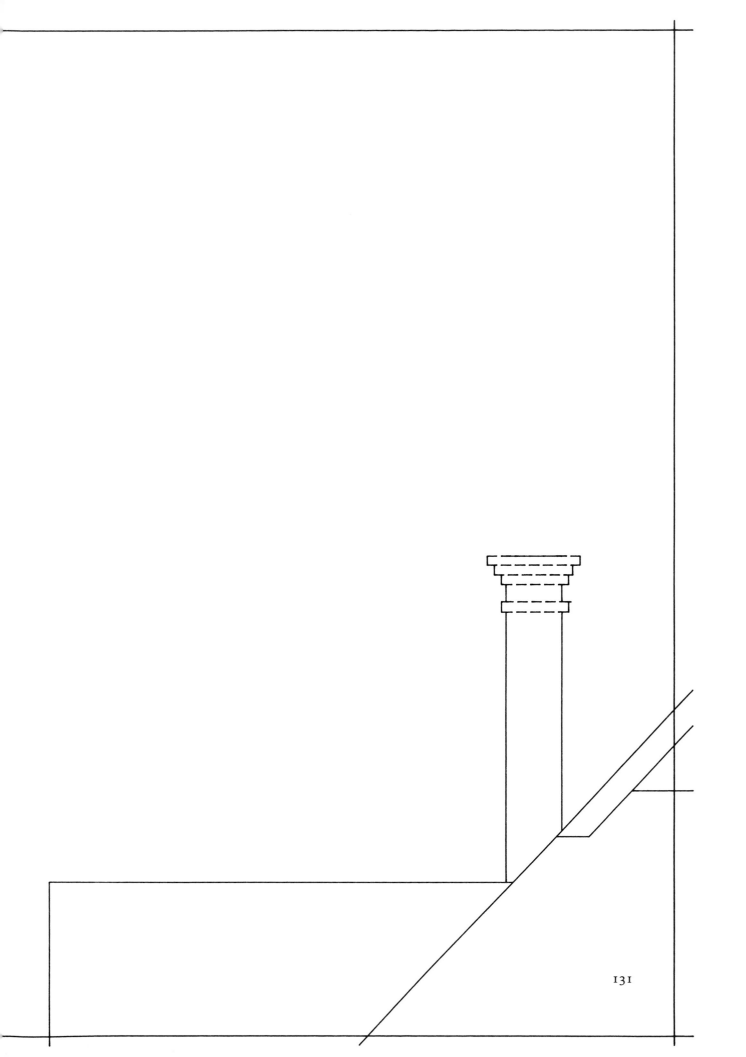

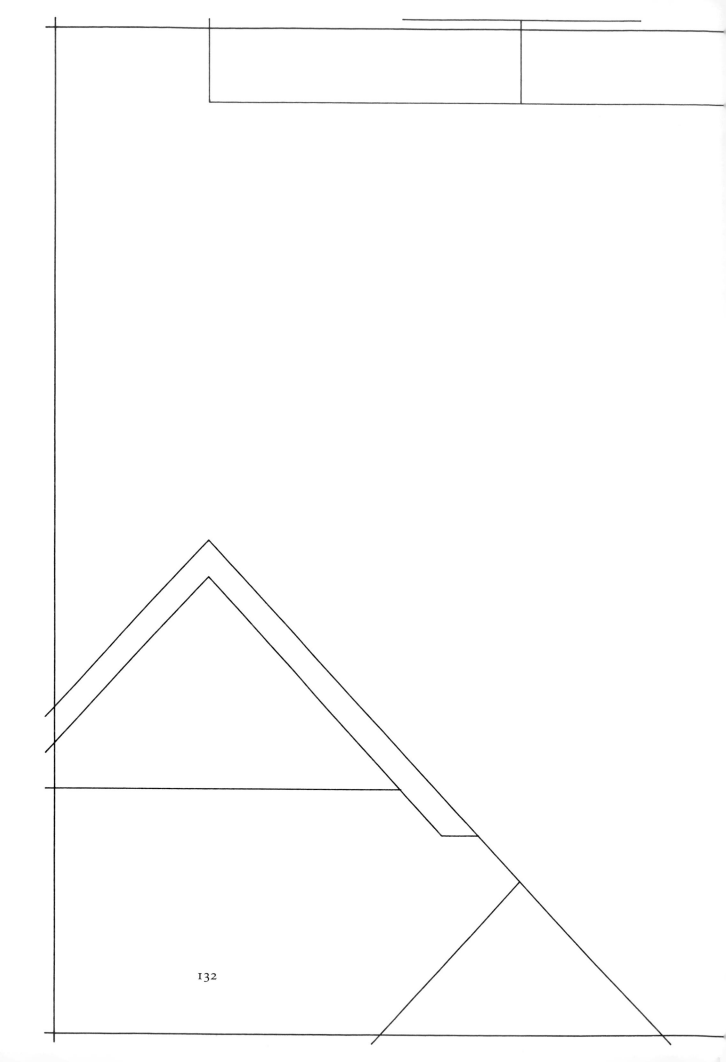

132

17

18

19

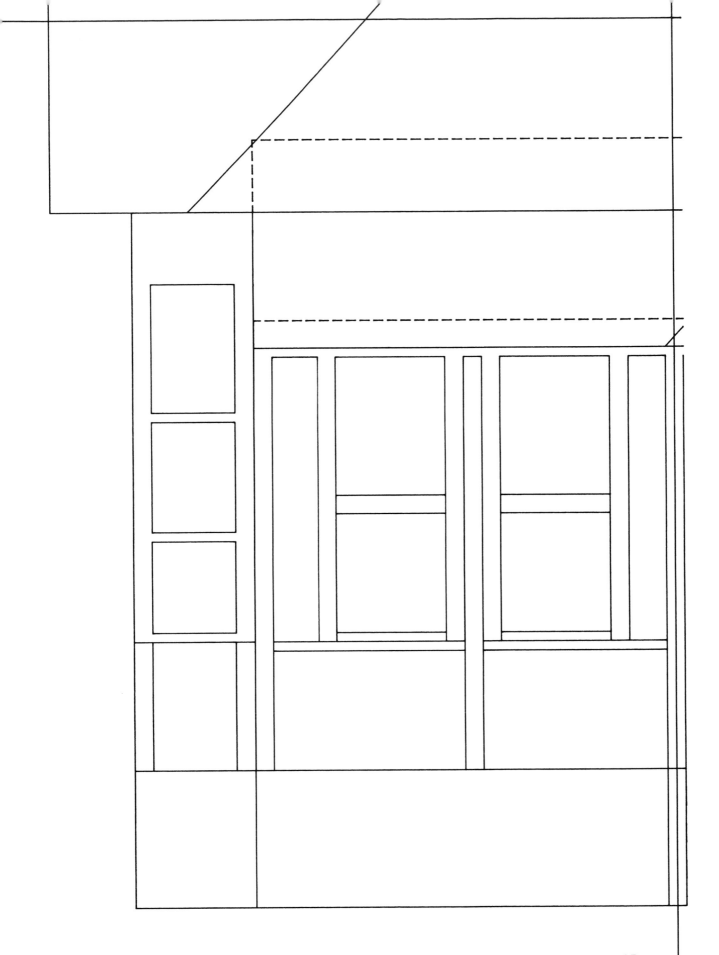

20

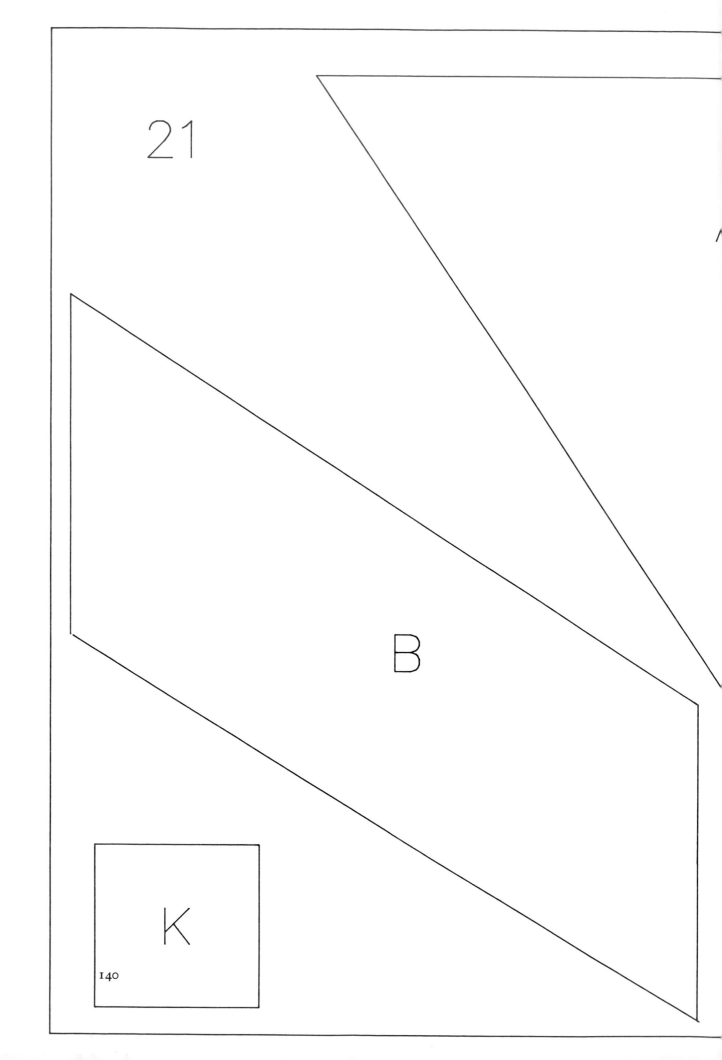

21

B

K

140

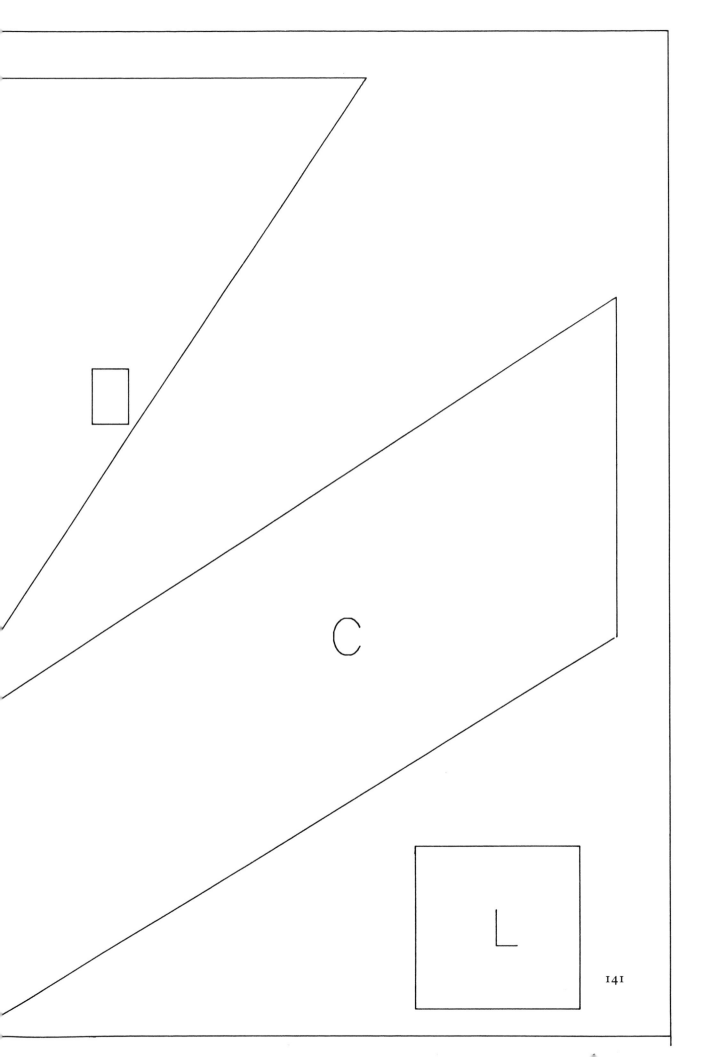

C

L

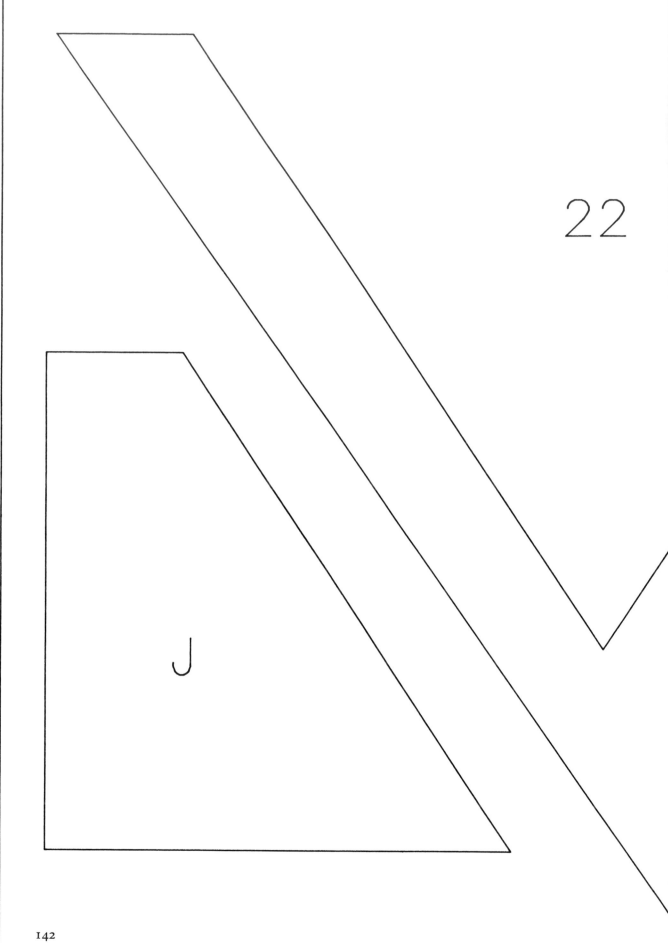

J

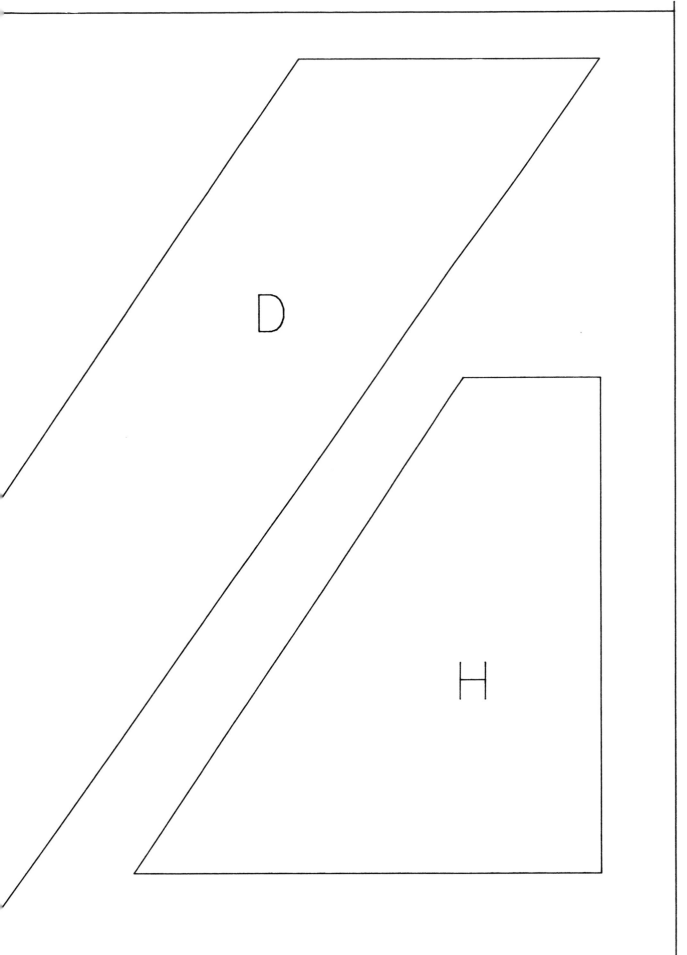

D

H

23

E

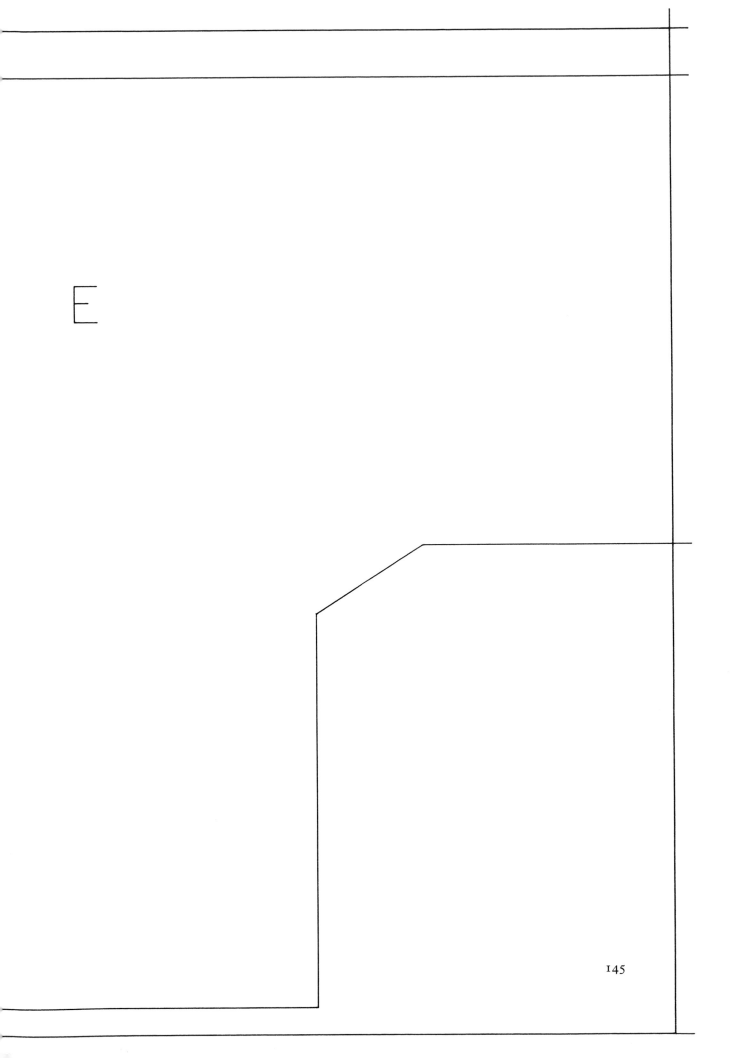

E

M

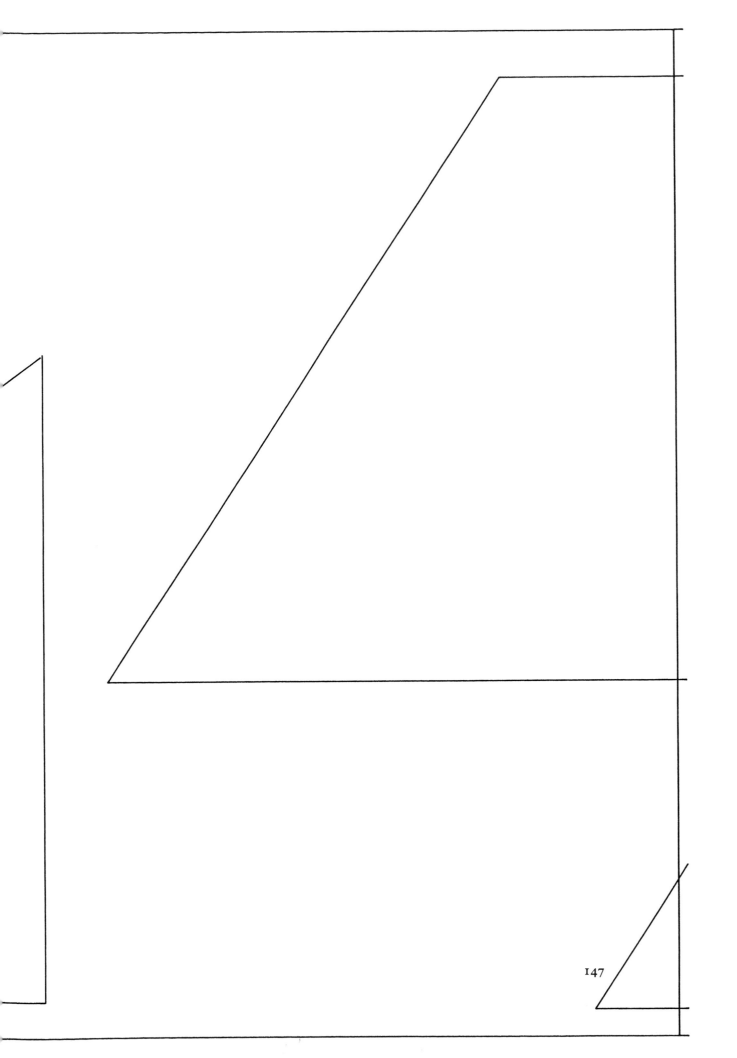

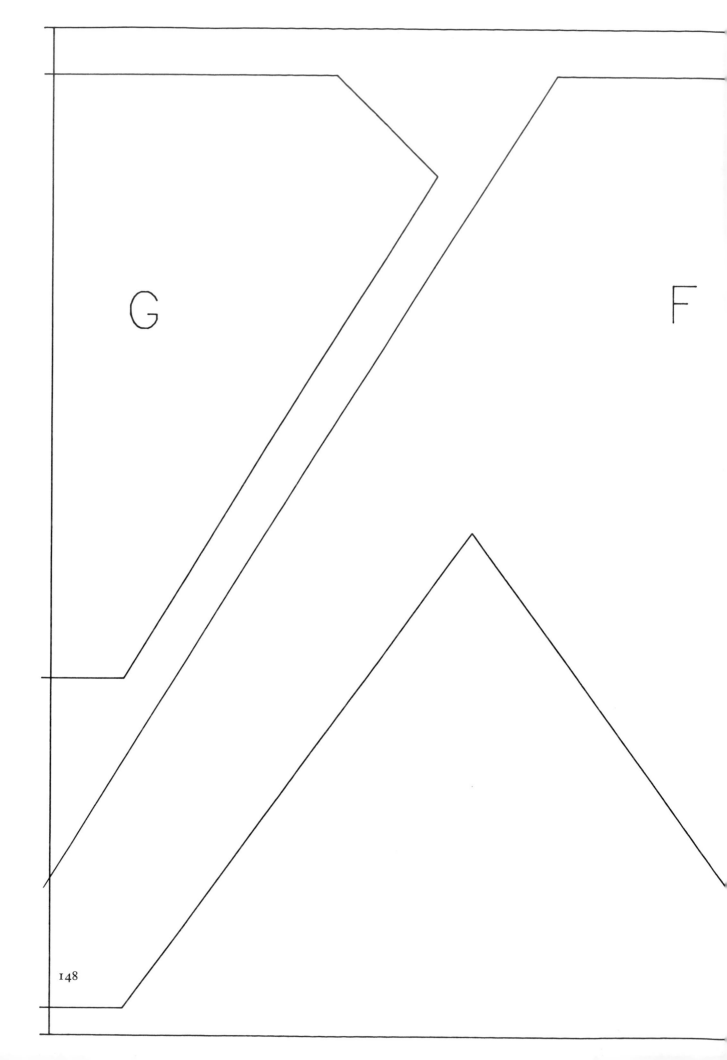

G

F

148

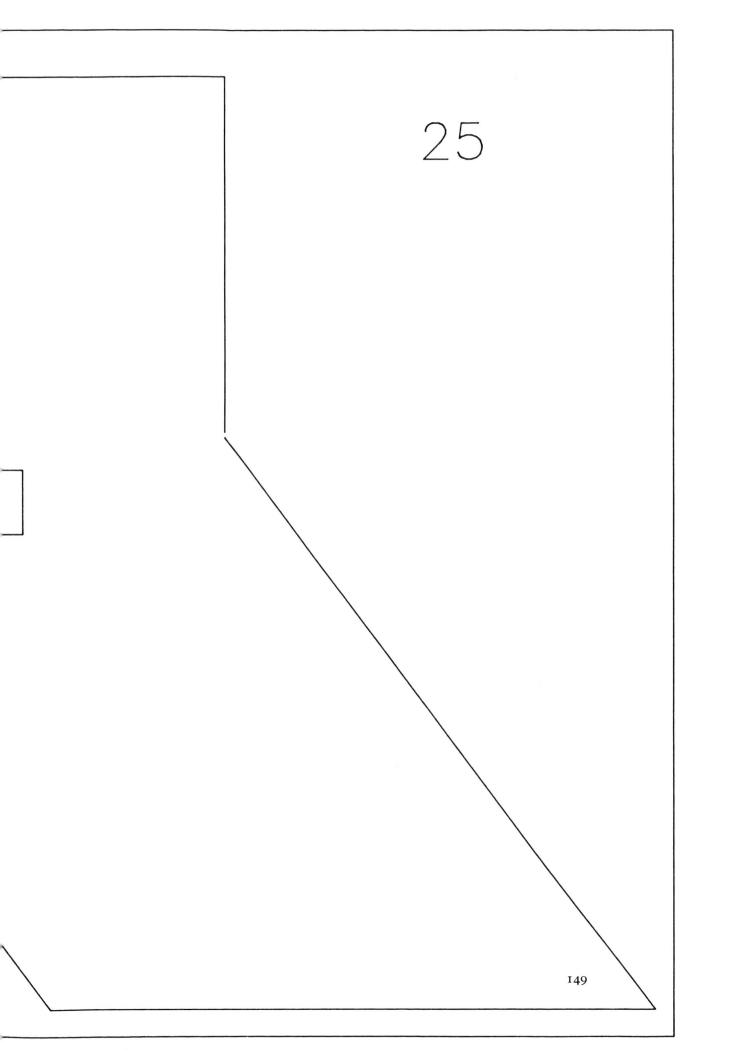